"God has always used young people. John Mark was only a teenager when he went with Paul and Barnabas on a missionary journey. Daniel and his three friends were all teenagers when they went to the ungodly foreign country of Babylon. *Be the Wave* will walk you into the lives of youth in the Bible who were heroes. As you look at their stories, you'll get answers for your challenges today. As you read, ask the Lord to make his ways a part of your everyday life of service."

—Loren Cunningham, *founder*, Youth with a Mission

"These are the young radicals of their day who dared to trust God, take on giants and overcome them in the pursuit of obedience to God . . . a brave young David, an innocent Mary and an anxious Esther. Their diaries leave behind an amazing legacy for the intrepid young warriors of today. The wave riders of this new generation are just as brave."

—Frank Naea, *director*, The WaveUSA

"I first met Rob Hensser in the dusty outskirts of Bombay, India. He had flown in to help train urban mission workers with Youth with a Mission. In the midst of the heat and oppression that is Bombay, Rob poured his life and heart into those students. The stories he told captured hearts as biblical principles were laid out. It was a life-transforming time. This book will do the same for you; it will capture your imagination and challenge your heart. Rob retells the stories of those young heroes in the Bible who have gone before us in the faith. Through their stories he places squarely in front of us the demands of modern discipleship. Read this book and be prepared never to be the same again!"

—David Lawton, *missions pastor*, Crossway Baptist Church,
    Melbourne, Australia

"*Be the Wave* challenges the emerging generation to embrace its destiny with clarity and creativity. Both young and old will be stirred to dream the dreams that connect them with the biblical trailblazers who heard and followed the call of God in their lives. This is a must-read for youth pastors and those they influence."

—Paul Trainor, *pastor of evangelism and mission*,
Central Christian Church, Las Vegas, Nevada

"Rob Hensser has written an enjoyable and challenging series of stories that will set you on a journey to fulfill God's destiny in your life. Rob lives out these principles and has a passionate desire to see a whole new generation live them out as well!"

—Steve Cochrane, *YWAM field director*,
South Central Asia

"*Be the Wave* disallows a compromised Christianity that doesn't believe in Hell but still thinks it's going to Heaven. Instead it reiterates in a relevant vogue what the love of God, revealed in Jesus Christ, demands. Read it and be challenged."

—Peter Parris, Fellowship of Connected Churches &
Ministries, Tallahassee, Florida

"Rob Hensser writes to the youth of today who find themselves more aware of the soon-coming time when they will hold the reins in their generation. By drawing from the lives of the youth of yesteryear who by faith made a difference, Rob encourages action, commitment and courage."

—Tom Hallas, Asia/Pacific *field director*,
Youth with a Mission

Be the WAVE

Daring to Believe God and Embrace Your Destiny

All Scripture quotations, unless otherwise indicated, are taken from the HOLY BIBLE, NEW INTER-NATIONAL VERSION®. NIV®. Copyright © 1973, 1978, 1984 by International Bible Society. Used by permission of Zondervan. All rights reserved.

Scripture quotations marked NLT are taken from the Holy Bible, *New Living Translation*, copyright © 1996. Used by permission of Tyndale House Publishers, Inc., Wheaton, Illinois 60189. All rights reserved.

Scripture quotations marked THE MESSAGE are taken from *The Message*, copyright © by Eugene H. Peterson, 1993, 1994, 1995. Used by permission of NavPress Publishing Group.

Cover and interior design by Brand Navigation
Edited by Dale Reeves and Jennifer Grosser

Library of Congress Cataloging-in-Publication Data:
Hensser, Rob, 1967-
      Be the wave : daring to believe God and embrace your destiny / Rob Hensser.
      p. cm.

    ISBN 0-7847-1766-4 (soft cover)
1. Youth—Religious life. 2. Christian life. 3. Bible—Biography. I. Title.
BV4531.3.H46 2005
248.8'3—dc22

                      2005002984

Printed in the United States of America.
refuge™ is a trademark of Standard Publishing
Standard Publishing, Cincinnati, Ohio.
A division of Standex International Corporation.

12	11	10	09	08	07	06	05
7	6	5	4	3	2	I	

ISBN: 0-7847-1766-4

Be the WAVE

Daring to Believe God and Embrace
Your Destiny

Rob Hensser

refuge™

an imprint of
Standard Publishing
www.rfgbooks.com

Dedication

Tricia, I owe you everything. Without you I am an empty shell struggling to overcome my hang-ups and misconceptions. Without your love, support and the thousand times you have read these chapters, this book would not exist. Any credit is yours, so this is dedicated to you.

Acknowledgments

Anyone who knows me knows that I owe them a huge debt that I could never repay. You have undoubtedly given much more to me than I could ever give to you.

Dale, and everyone at Standard Publishing, thank you for being open to God and giving me a chance. You embody the very spirit of God's heart to encourage and believe.

A special thanks to all the amazing Discipleship Training Schools I have had the absolute privilege of hanging out with (you know who you are). You are the inspiration for this book. Even as I write this, I am overwhelmed (it's hard to see the keyboard through my tears) by your talent, gifting, calling and most of all, your passion to live sold-out lives in outlandish pursuit of the Father. You are my inspiration—I love you and will always be there for you, anytime. Grab your destiny with both hands and *dare to believe!*

114081

Contents

foreword

A word from the wise—not necessarily old, but definitely wise. Isn't that what we all want? Encouraging, wise words from those who have followed after the ways of God from their youth, with all the usual challenges of growing up, mastering a whole heap of the big stuff on their way? Through their successes and failures, they have left us with their stories and an open invitation to come follow God as they and many other teenage daredevils have done.

What an amazing time in history to be alive! All the prophetic promises and challenges rise to meet us face-to-face, and another generation is asked the question, "Are you the wave?" We have been praying for the next wave to come, the next great outpouring of his Spirit—believing that God has said it and he will bring it to pass. Whenever I travel in Europe or North America, I hear, "It's coming from the North"; whenever I'm in Australia and New Zealand, I hear, "It's coming from the South"; likewise in other parts of the world, "It's coming from the East or West." The indigenous non-Western leaders are rising, the hidden army of women is taking its place in godly leadership, the new seed is growing as the emerging generation makes its way to the fore and the underground Chinese church will walk one by one out of China—the largest missions' movement in the history of the world.

The people in this book are the young radicals of their day who dared to trust God, take on giants and overcome them in the pursuit of obedience and the call of God. A brave young David, an innocent Mary and an anxious Esther—their diaries leave behind an amazing legacy for the intrepid young warriors of today. The wave riders of this new generation are just as brave, but are wisely looking for seasoned surfing companions who will launch out into the deep with them. There is instruction, correction and encouragement for every young Christian who knows the call of God as his goal and who is bold enough to walk in the footsteps of those who have gone before—those courageous enough to leave their stories for us to follow.

Each of us has an inward sense, a knowing that we are living in those days we call our destiny, where for such a time as this we find ourselves. The promise of God for this time is simply that he will pour out his Spirit on all flesh. Men and women from North and South, East and West, Asia and the tribes will emerge as an idea whose time has come. They will be a generation like none before, because they aren't *looking* for the wave—they *are* the wave!

They have come to such a time as this, and history is about to repeat itself. This new generation has come to echo the age-old challenge of the kingdom.

Stop looking around for it to come from someone else. Stand up and say to one another, "Christ in us the hope of glory—it's time to *BE THE WAVE.*"

Frank Naea,
director, TheWaveUSA

introduction

You are the hope of the future, the next wave! I believe one thing: I believe that you and your generation have the potential to impact the world and disciple nations like none other. I bet my life on it. You, not I, are the hope of the future, the hope of the kingdom—and you know what? The future has never been in better hands. God is salivating, licking his chops with huge expectation, waiting for you to explode into the world. Only one thing stands between you and the huge, crazy, epic destiny God has been dreaming of—you. The only limitation is whether you will dare to believe in God's desire and ability to use you, embrace your destiny and take your place as the next wave of history-shapers.

You may not realize it, but the Bible is full of young men and women just like you who struggled with family problems, insecurity, stereotyping and rejection—the same problems that plague and discourage us today. Many of the Bible's heroes were in their late teens to early twenties when God called them to change the course of history, but we view them through the "stained glass" of history as flawless saints who never struggled, rather than as young people who overcame their doubts and obstacles to walk into their purpose and calling. In the following pages you will feel the doubt and confusion of a young orphan girl, the tension of a dysfunctional family as a young man tried to follow God's call, and the insecure feelings of someone trying to live up to a parent's desire for his life—ultimately daring to believe God in furious trust. Each life story also speaks to a relevant issue. Things like: "How can I hear God's voice?" "What is God's will for my life?" and "How can I find my destiny?"

I believe you have huge dreams, wild hopes and more gifting and ability than any preceding generation. But more importantly, God believes in you. As you stand on the precipice of a thrilling adventure, the Father looks on, full of hope and confident expectation.

God has a huge, wild destiny for you. The Father's strategy has always been to use young people's zeal and uncompromising obedience, and nothing has changed! Dare to believe that he has a destiny for you beyond your wildest dreams. As you follow it you will disciple nations, impact generations and bring revival like we have never seen before. It will take a reckless faith, extreme trust and the willingness to die to self. As we give it all to find white-hot worship, we will find true fulfillment. Just like the characters in this book, you are the next wave of young leaders that God wants to raise up and release over the whole earth. You are the hope of the future, you have a passion for the genuine—and Jesus loves that! Dream crazy big dreams, give yourself away in love and do as you please.

—Rob Hensser

Chapter one

victory through forgiveness

Joseph

The shouting felt louder than usual. The whole house seemed to throb with rage. A plate smashed against a wall and shattered to the ground in pieces. Lara's parents were fighting again. Her earliest memories were of lying in bed listening to them shout and fight. But tonight there was fear in the air. Her big sister slid out of bed, walked out of their room and crouched at the top of the stairs. Lara followed. As they peered over the railing, they saw their mom in the middle of the living room. She was sitting on their dad's chest, holding a carving knife to his throat. The two girls huddled together as tears silently trickled down their faces. Their parents were in such a rage that it took several minutes for them to notice they were no longer alone. With the carving knife still pressed to his throat, Lara's dad carefully turned his head to face them. Quietly he whispered, "Kids, go and get the neighbors." Lara's mom didn't move an inch. She stared distrustfully at Lara's dad. With cold force she countered, "Don't you girls move." Dread rooted the girls to the spot as they now sobbed uncontrollably. Lara's family fractured and split soon afterward.

Joseph knew all about growing up in a dysfunctional family. His family could have been featured on today's daytime talk shows. Joe's mother, Rachel, had died when he was young. He only faintly remembered her beauty and grace. His sole comforts were images, feelings and his father's memories. His dad, Jacob, had adored Rachel. She was his reason for existence. He had given fourteen years of his life to win her. Now he was different. He had little time for Joseph and his brothers. He withdrew into his own

world of grief and mourning. He became an "absent father," always there, but never really present.

The family slowly began to crumble, becoming more and more dysfunctional. Joseph had lost his mother, but he had three stepmothers, none of whom much liked the others. They constantly fought to win Jacob's full devotion. The house was filled with stepbrothers and stepsisters, all with the same father but different mothers. Life was a constant state of pandemonium, day and night, with twelve stepbrothers from four different mothers fighting and bickering. Each mother was constantly spoiling and indulging her own children, who could do no wrong, and chiding her wicked, evil stepchildren. When the mothers did bother to intervene in the constant warring, who would they believe was to blame? Each boy would turn and run to his mom who would naturally believe her little angel to be completely innocent. It was always the children of those *other* women who were the troublemakers. It was a tough environment for young Joseph. When he fell and cut his knee, or felt ill in the middle of the night, his mom was not there to comfort him. To make matters worse, his dad openly played favorites, right in front of his brothers. Jacob tried to ease his grief by spoiling little Joe. They all knew the score—dad did not love them as much as he loved Joseph, the son of his beloved Rachel. His brothers were so jealous they hated him.

When his brothers saw that their father loved him more than any of them, they hated him and could not speak a kind word to him. **Genesis 37:4**

Just when it seemed things couldn't get any worse . . . they did. When Joe was in his mid-teens, his dad gave him a coat. That's no big deal; we all need a new coat from time to time—but this coat was more than just a coat. First, it was very expensive, more expensive than anyone else's coat.

It was made of the finest fabrics, with stunning colors and costly jewels sewn into it. That kind of coat was so expensive and magnificent that it was later reserved only for royalty. It was the sort of garment that the king would dress a princess in (2 Samuel 13:18)—although I'm sure Joe's was very manly. Beyond cost and appearance, the coat had a special meaning. The coat meant that Joe would lead the tribe after his father. Normally, a coat like this would have been given to the firstborn son, Reuben, but Joe was one of the youngest boys. Jacob had turned the family upside-down. One day Joseph's brothers, who hated the spoiled little pipsqueak, would have to bow to him!

Now Israel loved Joseph more than any of his other sons . . . and he made a richly ornamented robe for him. **Genesis 37:3**

His brothers seethed with envy and hate. They waited for the perfect moment to get revenge. Finally it came. They were tending the flocks in a remote part of the countryside—miles from home. They jumped on Joe. All of their anger and pain spilled out in torrents while they ripped the coat from his body. Holding their kid brother down, they spat in his face and took turns taunting and beating him mercilessly. They would get rid of him forever, and then Jacob would have to love them! When all of their rage was spent, they threw Joseph, naked and broken, into a deep hole that was used to collect water in the rainy season.

Without feeling or remorse they coldly sold their own brother into slavery. They laughed as they bartered away his life. Joseph's tears stung his eyes as they mingled with the blood. He shook with fear while he watched his brothers scoff and shout as he disappeared from view. Joseph screamed and shouted, shaking his cage. The cold night air blew against his exposed skin; he shivered and curled up into a ball. Tears flowed down his cheeks as

the cruel words of his brothers' rejection rang in his ears.

The simple moral fact is that words kill. Matthew 5:22, THE MESSAGE

When I was at school, we had a saying, "Sticks and stones may break my bones, but words will never hurt me!" That's not true. Often words, or the lack of words, hurt far more than physical pain. The internal scars caused by a friend or loved one remain long after any external bruise is gone. You probably know exactly what I mean. I'm sure you can remember a time when someone said something that was devastating. "You're a loser!" "You will never amount to anything!" "Who's going to want to be with you?" Or you can remember what was left unsaid. Your hurt may be the secret longing for a loved one to say "I love you. I'm proud of you."

The hurts you carry in life are "curses." A *curse* is any expression of rejection, spoken or unspoken. Joseph felt the deathblow of his brothers' curses as they rejected him and sold him into slavery. This kind of hurt is not always as dramatic as in Joseph's situation; a curse can slip out almost unnoticed. Have you ever longed for a loved one just to notice and affirm you? A curse is anything that makes you feel torn down rather than encouraged.

If you're like most people, the first thing you do when you are hurt is to get really angry. At the core of every hurt is a sense of loss. You have lost your sense of position or power; you may feel stupid or useless. The only thing to do is to try to regain control by getting angry. Anger gives a sense of power as you try to elevate yourself above the other person and regain control by tearing him or her down. When someone hurts you, you are probably tempted to swell up in fury and spout out a curse of your own. When my wife commented about my letter-writing skills, I immediately let her have it. "Yeah, what do *you* know? Remember the time you burnt that toast? Who do you think you are?" It's amazing what comes to mind in

the heat of anger, isn't it? What did burnt toast have to do with anything? It was just my attempt to regain control. My response of choice is a very mature phrase my little nephew taught me: "You're a stupid-head!"

OK, I realize my little nephew probably isn't the best source of wisdom for times like these. So what should we do when we feel hurt or rejected? The Bible tells us not to sin when we get angry. Feeling angry is not a sin. It happens. It's how we respond that matters. So how do we avoid sinning in our anger?

In your anger do not sin: Do not let the sun go down while you are still angry. **Ephesians 4:26**

I used to think this meant I could be really mad at someone all day. I could replay the incident over and over in my mind and enjoy my pity party. I could be rude and mean all day—as long as I forgave the person before I went to sleep. Because—let me be quite clear—I was the victim! I was as pure as the driven snow—wrongly accused. I'm such a nice guy, how could anyone say anything so hurtful to me? I deserved to be angry and mean, so I justified my actions. The other person was wrong, very wrong. As I replayed the incident over again and again, all the time I was thinking of new reasons why my persecutors were such sinners and I was so innocent. They were going to pay. They would have to come to me on their knees begging for mercy.

But this Scripture doesn't mean I can be angry all day and justify it. It means I should forgive immediately. If I don't forgive immediately it is SIN. The word *sin* literally means to "miss the mark." It's the picture of aiming for a bull's-eye on a target and missing. My target is to unconditionally forgive and accept others, just as God did me. When I get angry and don't forgive, I sin—I miss the mark. This gives the devil a foothold in my life.

Do not give the devil a foothold. **Ephesians 4:27**

The movie *Saving Private Ryan* is the true story of how Allied forces managed to take a small piece of beach on the coast of Normandy, France, during World War II. The day was known as D-Day. When the troops took that tiny sliver of land, they established a foothold in Europe. The enemy controlled the entire continent. The Allied troops had a few hundred feet of beach, but it was the beginning of the end of the war. In fact, that day the leader of England, Winston Churchill, went on national radio and said the victory was won, the war was over—it was just a matter of time until the mopping up was finished. It would be several months before the fighting ended, but that day the war was won. That's how important a foothold is.

The days blurred into weeks. Joseph was hauled through the wilderness tied behind a camel. The sun blistered his parched lips. Exhausted, he struggled to stand as the camels relentlessly dragged him through the sand. Reality began to hit him. His father was not coming. There was no one to plead his innocence or fight for his release. He was sentenced to a life of pain and loneliness.

His new master was an Egyptian politician. As time passed slavery matured the spoiled young boy into a hardworking, dependable young man. Just as Joe began to settle into his new destiny, the sharp sting of betrayal struck again. While his master, Potiphar, was away on business, Potiphar's wife tried to seduce Joseph. She was a powerful woman, used to getting what she wanted. Joe was just a slave—he meant nothing to her. She was only interested in using him for momentary pleasure, and then he would be tossed aside and discarded like a used paper towel.

How easy it would have been for Joseph to give in to this temptation and gratify himself. *Obviously God doesn't care about me*, he thought. *Why not sleep with her?* After all he had been through, didn't he deserve to think of himself? This

wasn't love; it was lust, instant gratification. Hadn't he earned it? Yes, in the world's eyes. But Joseph stood for what was right. He refused her and chose sexual purity. What did he get for his trouble? More pain. When her husband returned, the woman accused Joseph of coming on to her. Joseph was thrown into a stinking, rotten dungeon . . . without parole!

To make matters worse, Potiphar knew Joseph was innocent. He could have killed Joe on the spot; slaves had no rights. If Potiphar had really believed his wife, he would have mercilessly tortured and killed Joe to make an example out of him. But he had his image to protect, so he sentenced Joe to a lifetime in prison. Joseph sacrificed to obey God and ended up rotting in a filthy dungeon. If ever someone deserved to be angry and unforgiving, it was Joseph. Surely he had the right to hate his brothers, Potiphar, and God. But Joseph knew it was not a sin to be hurt—it was his response to the hurt that mattered. If he did not release forgiveness in his anger, the hurt would develop into envy.

Envy is an aroused feeling of hostility. Jacob hurt Joe's brothers by spoiling him. They became angry and didn't forgive. The foothold developed into envy as they judged their brother, condemning him and elevating themselves in their anger. "We are better than he is," they said to themselves. "I deserve that coat; it's rightfully mine!"

When you're hurt and don't forgive, you may replay the incident in your mind and justify why you are right and the other person is wrong, and so you condemn them. In reality, the moment you feel hurt you have a choice. You can humble yourself and release forgiveness, or harbor the curse and build on the foothold of envy as you elevate yourself to judge and condemn the other.

Look after each other so that none of you will miss out on the special favor of God. Watch out that no bitter root of unbelief rises up among you,

for whenever it springs up, many are corrupted by its poison.

Hebrews 12:15, NLT

If you miss the grace of God (forgiveness), a root will take hold in your heart. Roots go everywhere, and the longer they remain the harder it is to dig them out. After a period of time, envy becomes a "bitter root." By this stage, you will have convinced yourself that you don't have to forgive. You can deceive yourself with truth. Joseph's brothers used truth to justify their actions toward him and built a stronghold of bitterness on the foothold. It was wrong that their father gave such preferential treatment to Joe. Joe had acted like a spoiled brat and used his favored position to annoy his brothers. He could have given them more respect. This was all true, but it was applied to justify the sin of withholding forgiveness. When my wife hurt me, I had a choice. I should have immediately forgiven, but I didn't, and that allowed a foothold for the devil. Then I became envious, judging and condemning her to elevate myself in my anger. I used all sorts of truth. She had made mistakes; I had worked on the letter for a long time . . . yada, yada, yada!

At times like this I go straight to the top and try to get God to agree with me. I try to justify my actions to him. "God, you saw that, right? How could she do that? She's supposed to be a Christian! Lord, you know I would forgive, but she needs to learn a lesson. I pray that you will convict her and that she repents!" God, however, isn't buying any of it. He has only one thing to say to me, "Come on, son. Let's go and put it right."

If you enter your place of worship and, about to make an offering, you suddenly remember a grudge a friend has against you, abandon your offering, leave immediately, go to this friend and make things right. Then

and only then, come back and work things out with God.

Matthew 5:23, 24, THE MESSAGE

When you come into God's presence with a broken relationship that you are trying to justify or ignore, the Father gently whispers, "Let's go and fix it. Go and forgive. Seek reconciliation. Then I will receive your offering of prayer."

"But, God, you don't understand," I argue, "I would do that, but she needs to learn. You need to convict her and bring her to repentance. I would gladly forgive, but I am going to hold out and make our lives really miserable—for her sake!"

Yeah, right. Here's the bottom line: if I am not willing to forgive, I will not be forgiven.

If you do not forgive men their sins, your Father will not forgive your sins.

Matthew 6:15

It's not that God is unwilling to forgive. By my unforgiveness I actually tie his hands. I put myself where I cannot receive his grace. God is still willing to forgive, but I'm not interested. It's a bit like turning off a tap. The water is still running, but I have stopped it. When I don't forgive I throw God's mercy back in his face and refuse it.

Joseph's brothers betrayed him, his master abandoned him, and the butler who could have got him out of prison conveniently forgot him. If anyone deserved not to forgive, it was Joe. I mean, there is a limit, right? All this talk about forgiveness is well and good, but aren't there things that are unforgivable? Nope. Joseph could have held his hurt and built a stronghold of bitterness. He deserved to be mad at the world. But if he had been, he would have died in jail a bitter, twisted old man, and we never would have

heard of him. Joseph refused to allow the foothold in his life, and so he became a youth with a mission. As hard as it was, Joseph forgave his brothers,
Potiphar, the butler and God . . . right away. He released mercy, and God
used this teenager to change the course of history.

Joe had given up any hope of ever getting out of prison. He still
thought about the butler from time to time, but it had been two years
since he left. Joe lay on the floor in the corner of his cell and counted the
bricks in the ceiling. He knew there were 5,043. He had known there were
5,043 for years, but he checked them again every day just to be sure. He
was well into the 2,000s when the cell door clunked and creaked open. "On
your feet—it's shower time." Shower time? Joe didn't know anything about
shower time. They certainly hadn't had shower time recently—well, in the
last three to four years anyway. It felt so good to have the thick, scraggly
beard shaved from his face and his long, mangy hair washed and shaved.
He couldn't take his eyes off the mirror. He almost didn't recognize the
young man he saw there. He looked older, more worn—definitely a bit
wiser—than the boy he once knew.

"Get away from that mirror," the guard shoved him as he spoke. "It's
time to go before the great Pharaoh."

"Pharaoh?" Joe's mind began to swarm and swirl. *"Why am I going? . . .
The butler!"*

The butler must have finally remembered him. But could it be? It had
been so long. Joe felt hope rush through his body, but he tried to calm himself. He had been let down before, and he didn't want to get his hopes too
high. What on earth would he say to Pharaoh? He had rehearsed the speech
a thousand times, but now that the day to defend himself had arrived, he
didn't know what to think. Suddenly his defense seemed puny and full of
holes. Could he, a slave and a foreigner, really tell Pharaoh that his master's
wife had set him up? *What's the use?* he thought.

Joe was a little surprised to hear that Pharaoh had no idea about his

mishap with Mrs. P. and that frankly, he didn't care. He had bigger fish to fry.

"So what am I doing here?" inquired Joe as he waited to be called into the throne room. The future of a nation was to be decided that day, and the success of it hung on Joe. None of the royal counselors had been able to tell Pharaoh the meaning of a dream he had had the night before. Was Joe up to the task? Joe not only revealed the meaning of the dream, he came up with a plan of action to ensure the kingdom's survival. He didn't bitterly pronounce doom upon his captor; his forgiveness allowed him to seek blessing upon his adversary. When Pharaoh met Joseph he did not encounter a bitter young man with a chip on his shoulder. In fact Pharaoh asked,

Can we find anyone like this man, one in whom is the spirit of God?
Genesis 41:38

Wow! Wouldn't it be cool if people said that about you when they met you? God trusted Joseph to rule an empire and save millions of people from annihilation, including his own brothers who had mistreated him so many years before, and the nation of Israel, from whom the Savior of the world would come. In many ways the life of Joseph mirrors the life of Jesus—rejected by those closest to him, wrongly accused, his garments torn from him. Left in the prison of death, God resurrected Jesus and used him to save mankind. Willing and joyful forgiveness released both of them into their destinies to impact generations. Jesus prayed,

Father, forgive them, for they do not know what they are doing.
Luke 23:34

What will you do when you are hurt?

So from now on we regard no one from a worldly point of view. . . . All this is from God, who reconciled us to himself through Christ and gave us the ministry of reconciliation: that God was reconciling the world to himself in Christ, not counting men's sins against them. And he has committed to us the message of reconciliation. **2 Corinthians 5:16-19**

Reconciliation is not passive. It is not enough to say "I will forgive *if* they come to me and ask." It is active and immediate. Jesus forgave you while he was still on the cross. When you are still in the midst of your initial hurt, you must forgive.

Why forgive someone who has hurt you? The world will call you weak. People will take advantage of you. You could act tough and hold out, but if you do, in the end you will be the loser. Unforgiveness will plague your life. The root of bitterness will make everything taste bitter. Bitterness will keep you in an aggravated state of mind that inclines you to be harsh and irritable. It will make your whole demeanor sour as you try to ruin things for everybody else. You become a Super Grinch.

Have you ever noticed that bad guys in the movies are bad because someone hurt them? Someone, somewhere rejected them or did not recognize their talents, and now the world will be as miserable and full of pain as they are. When you refuse to forgive, you can experience things like depression, suspicion, paranoia, repression, insulation, isolation, anger, even physical ailments. Does that sound like winning to you? If it does . . . go for it!

The truth is that forgiveness is victory. It's not weakness or cowardice. It demands strength and courage. It's victory because the chains of bitterness fall off. You're set free and your relationship with God is clean and pure. But if you choose not to forgive, you are doomed to inherit the consequences.

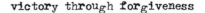
Any kingdom at war with itself is doomed. A divided home is also doomed.

Luke 11:17, NLT

The enemy wants to destroy relationships by dividing them. If you don't forgive you'll remain locked in a dungeon of bitterness that controls your life. Joseph was restricted but not imprisoned. Something is only a prison if you want to leave and can't. You could be imprisoned in a five-star hotel on Hawaii if you wanted to leave and couldn't. Joseph had forgiven. The chains had fallen from him, and he embraced his situation. His prison became his mission field.

Let's recap. When someone says or does something that hurts you, it is a curse that tears you down. At that moment of hurt you naturally become angry and try to regain control. At this point the Bible says you have a choice. Forgive, or hold onto your anger and establish a foothold for the devil. You build on your foothold as envy takes over. In time envy develops into a bitter root, as your foothold becomes an impenetrable stronghold of bitterness and unforgiveness. The stronghold will dominate your life and limit your impact on others.

How Do You Break Out of the Stronghold?

1. *See It*

The first thing to do is admit the pain, hurt or disappointment. Stop denying that it hurt. You may need to allow the Holy Spirit to gently lead you in this. Then confess it. Confessing simply means to agree with God. Agree with God that it hurt. Let him gently expose your heart. This is an emotional task.

2. *Free It*

Once you admit your hurt, separate the sin from the person. Jesus said,

Freely you have received, freely give. **Matthew 10:8**

This is an intellectual task. You consciously choose to release forgiveness and no longer hold the hurt against the person. This part of the process is not about feelings. It is a mental choice to say, "That hurt, but I forgive you, and I bless you."

3. *Leave It*

Be reconciled to the other person. It doesn't matter who started it or who is right or wrong. If you don't attempt to restore the relationship or release forgiveness, you are in sin. How often are you to do this? Check out Matthew 18:22—you are to do it every time. Here is a guideline for how to deal with a hurt. If it is private, keep it private. That means if someone hurt you but doesn't realize it (perhaps it was a remark or something left unsaid or undone), then just deal with it between you and God. Forgive the person and seek God's best for him or her. If it was public, deal with it publicly. That means if you had a big argument or disagreement, then go to the person, ask forgiveness and restore the relationship.

To forgive is not to forget—rather, it is to remember without malice.

True forgiveness is letting go—regardless of the other person's response. Don't go to a person and apologize because secretly you are waiting to hear, "Oh, it's all my fault." It's not true forgiveness if you're fishing for repentance. You have to be willing to ask for forgiveness even if the other person takes no responsibility. True forgiveness is humbly seeking reconciliation of a relationship and valuing it more than your pride. What is

more important, being right or having right relationships? Forgiveness will not always restore the relationship. You may forgive and apologize, and the other person may not receive it. That's OK. That's not your problem. You will be free. Don't wait until you *feel* like doing it. That day will never come, and the longer you put it off the deeper those roots will go. The stronghold will become a fortress that is harder and harder to penetrate.

4. *Live It*

Joseph gives us the key to living a life of radical forgiveness and freedom.

Don't be afraid. Am I in the place of God? You intended to harm me, but God intended it for good to accomplish what is now being done, the saving of many lives. **Genesis 50:19, 20**

So then, it was not you who sent me here, but God. **Genesis 45:8**

Whatever the circumstance Joseph found himself in, he realized the bigger picture. God was in control. Will you believe that whatever has happened is not too much for God to redeem or use? That doesn't mean God wants you to be hurt or for bad stuff to happen to you—of course he doesn't. But if you trust God, he'll bring hope and healing. Perhaps you've had a bad family situation, a bad relationship, you've been used or you just feel that bad things have happened in your life and God doesn't care. Trust him. He does care and he promises to use it for good (Romans 8:28) if we'll forgive and walk in obedience. Who knows? Perhaps a nation will be changed or the lives of millions impacted by a youth with a mission just like you.

Making Waves

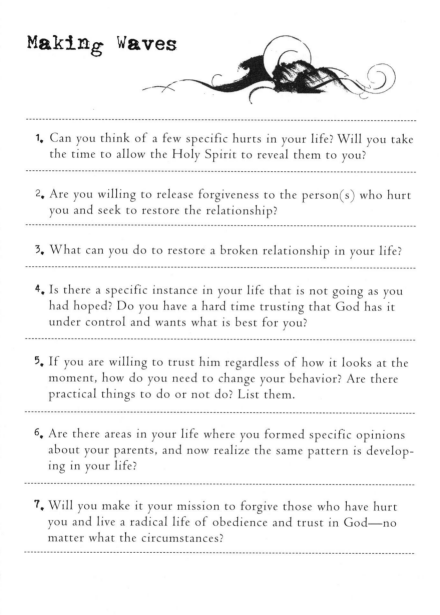

---

1. Can you think of a few specific hurts in your life? Will you take the time to allow the Holy Spirit to reveal them to you?

---

2. Are you willing to release forgiveness to the person(s) who hurt you and seek to restore the relationship?

---

3. What can you do to restore a broken relationship in your life?

---

4. Is there a specific instance in your life that is not going as you had hoped? Do you have a hard time trusting that God has it under control and wants what is best for you?

---

5. If you are willing to trust him regardless of how it looks at the moment, how do you need to change your behavior? Are there practical things to do or not do? List them.

---

6. Are there areas in your life where you formed specific opinions about your parents, and now realize the same pattern is developing in your life?

---

7. Will you make it your mission to forgive those who have hurt you and live a radical life of obedience and trust in God—no matter what the circumstances?

List three things God has shown you in this chapter that you don't want to forget.

1.

2.

3.

Be the Wave

Lord, from this moment on I commit to . . .

Spend a few minutes talking to God about how you feel. List some specific prayer points that will help you live out the truths in this chapter.

Chapter two

embracing your destiny

Gideon

They were out there . . . waiting! The sun hung motionless in the noonday sky, its heat pounding down relentlessly. Beads of sweat ran down Gideon's well-tanned face as the desert breeze blew the dust into it. Grimacing and spitting the grainy sand from his lips, he slashed and cut down the last stalks of grain. *This is useless,* he thought to himself in frustration. The harvest that year was pitiful. They had been able to plant only one small field and it was scraggly and feeble. Nervously, he looked to the foothills that stretched down toward him as if to engulf the farm in their grasp. Just on the other side he could see towers of smoke rising before vaporizing into the clear, hot sky. They would be here any day now.

"They" were the Midianites, a neighboring nation that had held Israel in their oppressive clutches for as long as Gideon could remember. But things had never been this bad. These people seemingly came from nowhere, like a swarm of locusts descending upon the land just as the last sheaves of grain had been brought in. Israel was still in its infancy as a nation. They had no national army or police force to look to for protection. The only things holding the nation together were frail tribal ties that were traced back to twelve brothers centuries ago. Nobody was really interested in helping his or her neighbor; everyone just looked out for number one—doing what was right in his or her own eyes. Totally unprepared for the invasion, Israel's makeshift volunteer guard had crumbled as quickly as it had assembled. Since that fateful time seven years ago, they had remained in bondage to the Midianites. They camped everywhere, ruining the land

and plundering livestock for food. Israel was left devastated. Each season people scraped together what grain they could to plant and grow food. But as soon as harvest was complete, a small detachment of Midianite soldiers would show up to rape, ransack and make off with everything. On and on this went . . . for seven years! Each year there was less and less grain to plant. Only a few people even bothered to plant grain anymore. Why go to the trouble of planting and working the field just to have it snatched away when all the work was done? People were losing hope. No one seemed to care.

Young Gideon harvested the meager crop, keeping one eye on the hills, watching for the enemy. They were out there somewhere. He felt hopelessness overwhelm him. *What's the point? Here I am sweating away and they are out there watching me, laughing. Why don't they just come and put me out of my misery?* He felt so small, so insignificant . . . so vulnerable. His heart pounded as he cautiously dragged the last of the harvest over to the barn. His nerves were tingling and his ears were on alert, listening for every faint sound. Where were they, his enemies? Were they just toying with him? It was agonizing.

Now what? he thought to himself. The idea of continuing his work seemed so useless, but what other choice was there? He could keep working or admit defeat and starve. He squinted in the bright sunlight as he combed the horizon with his eyes. *Where are they? Have they forgotten? Could they have overlooked this small corner of Israel?* A small spark of hope flickered in his heart. Perhaps there would be time to thresh the grain and finish; perhaps this year might be different, but he would have to act quickly if there were to be any chance of success. He looked at the flat, exposed threshing floor. *This is no good; someone will surely see me out here,* he thought. *I need a place to hide.* Nervously he looked around for the perfect place. His heart was pounding and his pulse racing as he scanned the area. A knot of anxiety thumped in his chest, making it hard to swallow. His mind raced with all sorts of thoughts. *There must be somewhere,* he chanted as he rubbed his blistered hand over his short prickly hair.

"That's it, the winepress!"

In Gideon's day a winepress was little more than a hole in the ground. At harvest time the grapes were thrown in and trodden on. While it was great for treading grapes, it wasn't the best place for threshing grain. Normally, threshing was done on a flat, exposed surface. All the grain would be thrown in a pile and beaten with sticks to make the kernels fall off the stalks. Then the stalks would be tossed in the air with a pitchfork, and the wind would blow the lighter stalk away while the heavier kernels fell to the ground. But if Gideon began doing all that out in the open, surely he would be seen.

Could this possibly work? he thought, sweat rolling into his eyes, his hands shaking. He threw his scanty harvest into the hole and then jumped in, disappearing from view. Gideon froze. He waited for what seemed an eternity, then slowly raised his head just enough to peer over the rim of the hole. The coast was clear, but had anyone seen him? He tried to convince himself that no one would notice him down there. Trying not to make a sound, he slowly began to thresh. Every now and again he stopped, carefully checked that the coast was still clear, then quietly went back to work. His heart pounded, the fear of being noticed filling his every thought. With every faint noise he pricked up his ears automatically and the hair on the back of his neck stood at attention. Suddenly, he heard something. His heart pounded so hard he felt faint; panic gripped his rigid body. He could feel someone's stare burning into the back of his neck. His body refused to turn and look; he closed his eyes in utter defeat. They were standing there—he just knew it. He would turn around to see Midianite soldiers smiling at him in his pathetic situation. Hopeless anger surged through his frame. He closed his eyes for a second, praying that they would disappear, then took a long, deep breath and slowly turned to face his enemy.

As he turned a bright light blinded him and seemed to physically shove him. He fell backward in the hole and sprawled across the grain. He knocked his head on the side of the hole and jammed his neck. A great weight appeared to be pressing down on him. The brightness seemed to burn through his eyelids and penetrate his skin. He squinted like a gunslinger looking into the high-noon sun. Slowly his eyes focused and he froze.

Gideon's knees shook. He mouthed words but nothing came out. He felt cold with fear. His whole body went into shock, and he curled up like a baby, trembling in desperation. There above him standing at the edge of the hole was the most awesome sight he had ever seen. Looking down on him was a shimmering, majestic, frightening angel of God. His brilliance hurt Gideon's eyes, and the noise of his wings was like earsplitting peals of thunder. He towered over the hole as if it would swallow everything in sight in one dreadful swoop. Gideon cowered backward, terrified. The sky itself seemed to be falling as the angel slowly spoke,

The Lord is with you, mighty warrior. Judges 6:12

Now, hang on a minute. That's kind of a strange thing for the angel to say. "Mighty warrior"? Those words make me think of an upset Klingon singing battle songs and dribbling his blood wine as he snarls, "Today is a good day to die!" Gideon doesn't remind me of a mighty warrior. He's a wimp—hiding in a hole in the ground. Did this angel make some mistake?

Did he take a wrong turn somewhere?

Was he supposed to be at some other hole?

Did he get bad directions?

There was nothing mighty or warrior-like about this young man hiding in a hole, sucking his thumb and crying for his mommy. So what's the deal?

When the angel greeted Gideon, he proclaimed *God's perspective.* You see, when God looked at this young man he saw his destiny—not how he was, but how he would be! That's how God looks at all of us.

Remember, dear brothers and sisters, that few of you were wise in the world's eyes, or powerful, or wealthy when God called you. Instead, God deliberately chose things the world considers foolish in order to shame those who think they are wise. And he chose those who are powerless to shame those who are powerful. 1 Corinthians 1:26, 27, NLT

Nobody that God calls has it all together. God enjoys using weak failures. None of us deserves his mercy and grace. But the good news is that God does not focus on where we are. He looks at us from outside of time and sees us in our destiny.

Just like Gideon, each one of us has a divine destiny. You have a purpose, something that God has called you, and only you, to do. Whether you realize it or not, there is a specific role that God has for you to play in bringing his kingdom into the world. Only you have just the right combination of skills and divine calling. If you don't do it . . . it won't be done. Stop for a minute and think about what you want to do for God. Dream the biggest dream you can imagine. Got it? Is it outrageously big? Way bigger than you could accomplish on your own? Well, you haven't even begun to scratch the surface of God's dream for you. Check this out:

No eye has seen, no ear has heard, no mind has conceived what God has prepared for those who love him. 1 Corinthians 2:9

God has destinies for us that are beyond our wildest dreams. Now, I can dream some pretty wild dreams! I am a daydreamer from way back. I spend hours sitting around thinking about what I want to do, how I want to impact the world. But as big and as awesome as my dreams are, they don't even come close to God's. God has a destiny for you and me that's

AWESOME! This is what he says about your future:

For I know the plans I have for you . . . plans to prosper you and not to harm you, plans to give you hope and a future. **Jeremiah 29:11**

He sees *you* as a mighty warrior! I think the apostle Paul had this in mind when he prayed,

I pray also that the eyes of your heart may be enlightened in order that you may know the hope to which he has called you, the riches of his glorious inheritance in the saints, and his incomparably great power for us who believe. That power is like the working of his mighty strength, which he exerted in Christ when he raised him from the dead.
Ephesians 1:18-20

As we realize the truth of how God sees us, we are filled with hope. We begin to receive our inheritance and live a confident, purpose-filled life of power. If you have read the Gospels, you know that Jesus did some amazing stuff. He healed the sick, stilled storms, multiplied food, cast out demons, walked on water and raised the dead. But the greatest miracle of all was his resurrection from the dead. Paul says the same resurrection power is available to us, now. Do you really believe that you could do all the things that Jesus did and more? God does.

I tell you the truth, anyone who has faith in me will do what I have been doing. He will do even greater things than these, because I am going to the Father. **John 14:12**

All we have to do is trust him and walk in obedience.

Gideon wasn't acting or feeling much like a mighty warrior at the time, but it was still true. Regardless of how we feel or how we've been acting, it's true for us too. God has more faith in us than we have in ourselves. He is filled with expectation for our lives . . . he's bursting with excitement and hope. He has faith in you. He doesn't see our hang-ups, goof-ups or let-downs. When he looks at us he doesn't even notice most of the junk we're afraid of. He sees mighty warriors. He sees us as we will be in our destiny.

Gideon stared at the angel blankly. The silence was deafening. An age seemed to pass. "Have you lost your mind? Mighty warrior? Where?" he finally blurted out.

He looked around the hole. "There are no mighty warriors here . . . just me. Are you sure you have the right hole?"

Gideon's perspective was radically different from God's. He saw himself as the wimpiest of all the wimps. Here's what he said:

If the Lord is with us, why has all this happened to us? Where are all his wonders that our fathers told us about when they said, "Did not the Lord bring us up out of Egypt?" But now the Lord has abandoned us and put us into the hand of Midian. . . . But Lord, how can I save Israel? My clan is the weakest in Manasseh, and I am the least in my family. Judges 6:13, 15

Gideon looked at the angel in utter disbelief. He seemed to have completely forgotten he was conversing with a terrifying angelic creature. His disappointment and sense of hopelessness welled up within him. Frustrated tears filled his eyes as he shot back, "If God is with me, why am I struggling to find him? I pray and nothing ever seems to happen. I read the Bible and it is dry and boring. God speaks to everyone else around me, but not to me. I pray and it seems like my prayers don't make it past the ceiling.

Work is killing me, my family doesn't understand what I am doing . . . it's hard, confusing and overwhelming. Sometimes I look up to the heavens and I'm not sure if God even cares! And besides . . . I am the least. I'm nobody, just a kid. Why would God bother with me anyway? I'm not educated or experienced—nobody ever trusts me with anything."

To be honest, that's my perspective of myself most of the time. How about you? Have you ever thought, as Gideon did, "I'm too young, too weak, totally unprepared . . . I don't even know how to hear God's voice, if he does speak. Why would God speak to me anyway? I am just a kid, what do I know? God will use an adult." We have an incredible destiny and a purpose that is ordained by God. But there are two things that will steal our destiny from us. The first is a wrong perception of God (he isn't interested in me). The second is a wrong perception of ourselves (I'm a wimp).

Gideon felt that God was distant and uninterested, that God had abandoned him. I know how he feels. Sometimes I wonder if God is out there at all, and if he is, whether he listens to someone as unimportant as I am. Is God really interested in my problems compared to those all over the universe? I hear stories of God doing incredible things in other people's lives . . . but that sort of stuff doesn't happen to me. That's how Gideon felt. He grew up hearing the stories of how God had delivered the nation of Israel from Egypt, the greatest superpower in the known world. He heard the stories of how the great walls of Jericho fell at the sound of a shout. But that was a long time ago. Where was God now? Why didn't he deliver them from Midian? Why didn't he provide food for his starving family, or supernatural crops instead of the pitiful harvest he now stood on?

"I've heard the stories," shouted Gideon, "but where is God now? Does he even care?"

For years I allowed a wrong view of myself to keep me from my destiny. I grew up in a broken home and was plagued with feelings of guilt and shame. My parents were in love before I came along—that's why they

got married. Then as soon as I was born, they stopped loving one another and got divorced. Was it my fault? My dad moved away—didn't he love me? Was it something about my looks, my shape or my personality? These fears haunted me. Would anyone accept me for who I was if my own parents couldn't? Just like Gideon, I ran for security and protection by hiding, until finally, one day God pulled me up out of my hole to see myself as he sees me. He loves me as I am. He doesn't love me in spite of all my junk. He loves me *with* all my junk. Anything else would be conditional love and acceptance. Our greatest enemy to fulfilling our destiny is a wrong perception—of God or ourselves.

I am the only Christian in my family. My dad is a genius. He is a born leader. When he walks into a room everyone looks to him. If he had chosen to follow after God's heart, I am sure my whole family would have followed and become Christians. I have an elder brother. He is the most likable guy you will ever meet. Everyone loves him. He is the life of the party. If he had decided to follow Jesus, I would have followed in his footsteps, along with many others. Compared to my dad and brother, when I look at myself I see so many failures and disappointments. I feel unable—unqualified. But God can use everything that has happened in our lives in fulfilling our destinies.

And we know that God causes everything to work together for the good of those who love God and are called according to his purpose for them.

Romans 8:28, NLT

God has been preparing us from the foundation of the earth. No, it was not his desire for all of the stuff we have been through to happen, but he can redeem those things. He can use them for good. What I see as weakness, God sees as potential strengths. But the enemy will try to steal the benefits by convincing us that we are useless and that God is not interested.

Thankfully, God has more faith in us than we have in ourselves—he works with unpromising recruits.

The angel of the Lord (who many biblical scholars believe was an appearance of Jesus before his human birth) listened very politely as Gideon poured out his heart and his frustrations. Then when he was finished the angel replied,

---

Go in the strength you have and save Israel . . . I will be with you.

Judges 6:14, 16

This time Gideon threw up his arms to signal his frustration.

"Hang on just a minute! Have you not been listening to a word that I have said? I have just spent the last thirty minutes carefully listing all the reasons why *I have no strength!*"

Did God check out for a moment while Gideon explained exactly why he had no strength and why he was the wrong guy for the job? Didn't he understand? Gideon had just explained, quite clearly, that he was the weakest of the weak. A self-proclaimed wimp, a little guy. What didn't God understand about that? Go in the strength he had? In Gideon's mind he had *no* strength—he was a weakling. That's just about how I feel most of the time as well. I feel like I have no strength, no confidence. Surely there is somebody out there who is much more qualified, better prepared, more confident. You too may feel like you are the least of the least. Perhaps you lack confidence, strength or ability. You know what? That's OK with God. All he requires is that we are willing and obedient—to go in the strength we have.

I will be with you, and you will strike down all the Midianites together.

Judges 6:16

God will be with us all the way. If we are simply willing and obedient, he promises to be with us. Even if you feel like you have no strength, just go. Seize your destiny and he will be with you. It is not your *ability* but your *availability* that counts. As we step out in faith, we find his power and resources are ours. When we come to the end of ourselves, we are in the perfect place for God to work. So often we wait for God to be with us before we step out to follow hard after him. We have prayer meetings and intercession times. If only God will come and be with us, then we will move out and change the world or right a wrong. God doesn't tell us to wait for his presence and then we will feel empowered and equipped to go. He doesn't promise to come upon us and transform us into superheroes who know no fear or limitations before we step out in faith. He tells us to get going and then he'll be with us. If we want God to be with us, then we need to get going. We need to step out into those wild and crazy dreams God has put into our hearts, and he will be with us all the way. That's the promise.

Back to Gideon. There was one last piece of business. The Lord challenged him, saying,

Tear down your father's altar to Baal and cut down the Asherah pole beside it. Then build a proper kind of altar to the Lord your God.
Judges 6:25, 26

Gideon had to break free from the influence of those who were older in his family and embrace his own calling—no matter the consequences. He had to come out of the shadow of the adults in his life and follow God's unique call, embracing a new move of God.

Late that evening Gideon sat leaning against a tree and looked around. The sun glowed deep red as it slowly faded behind the foothills. The events from earlier that day swirled around in his mind. Was it real or just a dream?

Now that the angel was gone, his feelings of confidence and commitment began to ebb away. Fear and uncertainty rushed through his body. He shivered in the cool of the evening. Hour after hour passed as he sat and stared at the family altar and the Asherah pole beside it. (An Asherah pole was used for the obscene worship of a false goddess of several pagan nations.) How could Gideon dare tear it down? What would his father say? What would his elder brothers do? The words of the angel had seemed so inspiring, but now he was gone and Gideon was alone. He was just a youth. His father would not understand. Who was he to stand up and tell his family that they were all wrong? How could he tell his father that he was not going to go to college and get a "good job"? How could he face his family and tell them that he was not going to follow the same path as they had? He imagined their anger and disappointment—how could they ever understand? He could already hear their words ringing in his mind. He could feel his confidence shrink as he thought about all the obstacles.

"But God, I'm just a wimp," he protested. Then Gideon stood up. *Well, it's now or never.* He took a deep breath and walked over to the rough stone altar. Suddenly he heard a rustling. His face turned pale as he spun around on his heels. *What was that? Everyone must be asleep by now.* He stared into the night, straining his eyes to focus in the dark shadows. One of the dogs tossed around in a pile of hay before drifting back into a deep sleep. Gideon's heart was pounding so loud he couldn't hear anything as he picked up an axe from the woodshed. He stood in front of the altar, closed his eyes and swung with all of his might. The altar began to crumble and break. Again he swung, faster and faster, praying he would finish before anyone would hear and discover him. He pulled down the Asherah pole. His body was pumping with adrenaline, partly from fear and partly from excitement. Carefully he sifted through the rubble and reused the rough stones to build an altar to God. There was no going back now. He would no longer follow in the shadow of others . . . he would embrace his own destiny.

Sometimes the first hurdle to embracing our destiny is our own family. Regardless of how much your family loves and supports you, they're going to be worried. When I first told my family I was going to be a full-time missionary, they were anxious and said things like, "Why not choose a career using your degree, have a solid income, provide security for your family and do this 'other thing' on the side? You need to be more responsible."

They said these things out of love—they just wanted the best for me—but sometimes good ideas get in the way of God's ideas. Many people have heard the call of God's destiny only to give in to the pressures of family desires and guidance. Often the people who love us the most hinder us from embracing our purpose. We excitedly tell them how God has called us to embrace our destiny and see his kingdom impact lives, only to get the response, "How will you do that? Why do you want to go to China—aren't there lost people here in our town? Just teach Sunday school for a while and get this out of your system; then you can get on with your *real* future. At least get an education first so you have something to *fall back on*." Do we have such a lack of faith in God's calling that we need something to fall back on? What if that doesn't work out—do we have a fall-back for our fall-back? Jesus knew all about these pressures.

If anyone comes to me and does not hate his father and mother, his wife and children, his brothers and sisters—yes, even his own life—he cannot be my disciple. And anyone who does not carry his cross and follow me cannot be my disciple. Luke 14:26, 27

Wait a minute! Did Jesus really mean we must *hate* our moms? Of course not. He was saying our love, devotion and commitment go to him before parents, family, even ourselves. If we will trust him, we will not be disappointed.

And everyone who has left houses or brothers or sisters or father or mother or children or fields for my sake will receive a hundred times as much and will inherit eternal life. **Matthew 19:29**

Just as Gideon did, we have to come out of the shadows of our families and embrace our own destinies! We cannot worship at the altar of good ideas. We have to follow the Lord our God. We have to go.

Many years after Gideon a ragtag bunch of young guys from Galilee were filled with the same doubt. The disciples were spending a weekend camping in the Galilee hillside. The risen Jesus was in their midst and they worshiped him. But when it came to their destiny they still doubted. It was up to them now—they had to step out as mighty warriors, but they still felt like wimps. Jesus spoke the same hauntingly familiar words the angel spoke to Gideon. "Go . . . go in the strength you have, and I will be with you."

Go and make disciples of all nations. . . . Surely I am with you always.
Matthew 28:19, 20

We know these verses as the Great Commission. God has a destiny for us, a *co-mission.* God could snap his fingers and complete everything he desires to do, but he has chosen to do it with and through us. Why? Because embracing our destiny and partnering with God is the most dynamic, exciting, fulfilling mission we will ever embark on. Jesus defined Christians as people who go. People who leave their holes and embark on the most daring, thrilling, amazing and overwhelming adventure in life. It's beyond our wildest dreams! You may not feel ready—that's OK. Just be willing. God will be with you, mighty warrior!

Making Waves

1. Can you identify any times when you have done what seemed to be a good idea, but it wasn't God's idea?

2. Do you feel trapped serving a good thing (goal, career, plan, purpose) that is not God's best? How can you change it?

3. What is your perspective of yourself? Are you comfortable with the ways things are? What does the Bible say about how God sees us?

4. What do you think your relationship with God is like? Does he seem remote or uninterested? What does the Bible say about this?

5. Do you really believe God has been preparing you from the foundation of the world and can use your past failures or difficulties? Will you trust him to use them?

6. What do you think is God's destiny for your life?

7. Are you willing to forsake all for your destiny? Would you give up your own plans? What could you do to help your family understand?

8. Are you willing to embrace your destiny and trust that God will be with you? Will you commit your future to him now in prayer?

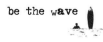

List three things God has shown you in this chapter that you don't want to forget.

1.
_____

2.
_____

3.
_____

Be the Wave

Lord, from this moment on I commit to . . .

Spend a few minutes talking to God about how you feel. List some specific prayer points that will help you live out the truths in this chapter.

_____
_____
_____
_____
_____
_____
_____
_____
_____

holiness that hurts the eyes

Ruth

Renee was breathtakingly beautiful. Every guy at church dreamed of asking her on a date. Her dark brown eyes sparkled with innocence. When she walked, she seemed to float on a wave of joy and pure love of life. Since graduating from high school six months ago, she had been working full-time. That's when she noticed Dan. His dark, wavy hair was swept back, and he had an exotic accent that made him sound like a movie star. There had been moments when Renee caught herself daydreaming about being on a date with Dan, but now it was real. It hardly seemed possible; before this night they had exchanged only a few casual words in passing, but now they sat, leaning over their dessert, talking about everything from childhood to the local sports team. Even though she had known him for only a few hours, the conversation flowed naturally and easily, as if they were old friends. There wasn't a single awkward moment of silence the whole night; it seemed they would never run out of things to say.

Over the next few weeks, Dan and Renee spent their evenings talking, walking in the park and driving around town in his little, red convertible. Dan intrigued Renee, but an uneasy feeling had been growing in the pit of her stomach. Over the past few evenings, it had become clear to Renee that Dan was not a Christian. Renee discussed it with her parents over dinner one night. Her mom and dad confirmed what she knew in her heart. She had to stop seeing Dan.

Her heart pounded nervously in her chest as they sat on a bench by the river. They chatted for a while, but Renee knew she couldn't keep putting

it off. She took a deep breath and mumbled, "Dan, I'm really sorry, but I can't see you anymore." A tear welled up in her big, dark eyes and her lip quivered gently as she spoke.

Dan's face betrayed his feelings of shock and fear. "Why?"

Renee choked back her tears and slowly explained that she was developing feelings for Dan but that, as a Christian, it was not right for her to pursue a relationship with a nonbeliever. Dan looked at her intently. Her face was scrunched up like a little rabbit's as she fought back a tide of emotions. The silence was getting louder and louder as they stared awkwardly at one another. Finally Dan shattered the silence, "What exactly do you believe?"

Renee was a little startled; of all the scenarios she had played in her head, this hadn't been one of them. She snapped herself back to attention and thoughtfully answered Dan's questions. After several hours of intense conversation, Dan looked up from the picnic bench he sat straddled across. "I believe everything you have said . . . I guess I've just never thought of it like that before."

Now Renee was really panicking. This was definitely not going as she had imagined. "I think you should come and talk with my dad," she whispered, gnawing her bottom lip.

It was late as they sat around the dining room table, but Dan listened intently as Renee's dad talked about Jesus. He seemed to soak it up, like a bone-dry sponge absorbs water. Later that night Dan lay in bed, staring at the ceiling, trying desperately to keep everything he had heard straight in his mind. Dan had met Christians before, but regardless of what they said, they were all pretty much just like him. Renee was different. She seemed to really believe what she said and was willing to live out her convictions even if it hurt. Her consistent example spurred Dan on his own journey of discovery about Jesus. Three weeks later he knelt before Jesus and gave him his heart and his life.

Renee lived a lifestyle of holiness. That extreme stance impacted Dan and was the beginning of his journey to salvation. Today Dan and Renee are more in love than the day they married and are radically living for Jesus as foreign missionaries.

A caravan of dusty camels slowly glided by the well as Ruth leaned over, struggling to hoist the water bucket up. She stopped to catch her breath, balancing the bucket on the rim of the well, and watched intently. The family looked defeated and dejected as they shuffled alongside the camels. Where were they from? Where would they pitch their tent? The desert seemed crowded because so many people had moved there recently. Times were definitely changing. Ruth was too young to understand all the reasons, but she knew it had something to do with the recession and famine her father kept complaining about. Every family that moved into the neighborhood spoke of the difficult times back home. That's why they were coming to Moab. They were hungry.

Ruth's great-grandfather had first settled here in the desert close to the river Arnon. Her family grazed their few sheep and goats in the scrub that grew on the riverbanks and traded milk, cheese and wool with the traveling merchants who came from distant, exotic lands—following the main trade route from Mesopotamia down to the Great Continent. Ruth loved to watch the long convoys of traders when they passed. She stared at their skin, dark as the night, their clothes glowing with stunning colors in the high Eastern sun. As she watched, she would imagine the exotic places they were from, places with great oceans, strange foods and bizarre animals living in the trees. Ruth would sit and watch for hours, dreaming of life in her distant fantasylands.

Life in Moab was boring. It was like lukewarm soda on a hot day, like sausage without any spice, like cake baked without sugar. Everything in the desert was the same sun-bleached shade of . . . blah! There were no trees to climb, no green grass to roll and play in—just dusty, dry desert. Everyone who lived on the trade route struggled to eke out an existence, barely surviving from one day to the next. To make things worse, a terrible famine had struck the neighboring nation of Israel, and many families had been driven from their barren homes in an attempt at survival. Every week it seemed a new family, gaunt with hunger and drained of energy, settled in the area with hopes of trading and surviving. The arrival of each new dust-covered, exhausted family would only bring more tension and discontent among the Moabite people settled on the riverbanks.

Israelites couldn't be trusted. At least, that's what everyone Ruth knew said. There was a long history between these two peoples, and none of it was happy. Both nations traced their heritage back to the same man: a Bedouin named Abram. Moab, however, descended from Abram's nephew Lot who, in a drunken haze, had slept with his own daughters, resulting in a child they named Moab. Moab rejected the God of Abram and served a fertility god, Baal of Peor, whose worship often included sexual immorality and temple prostitutes. Neither nation trusted the other, which often led to war. Many years before, when Israel had returned to Canaan from Egypt, the king of Moab tried to put a curse on Israel. When that failed he sent Moabite women to entice the Israelite men into idolatry and sexual immorality, and it worked. More recently the tribes of Reuben and Gad had driven many Moabites from their land, taking it for their own inheritance. *Israelites couldn't be trusted.* At least, that was what Ruth had heard.

Ruth carefully poured the cool, clear water into the large, clay jar that sat in the shade under a generous canopy that extended from the front of the tent. In the afternoons Ruth would sit in its shade and help her mother knead the dough for the evening flatbread. Pulling back the heavy skin tent flap she squeezed inside. It took a couple of seconds for her eyes to adjust to the dusky, dimly lit interior after the glaring brightness outside. Who were these strangers sitting and talking with her father? One of the men looked

familiar, and Ruth wracked her memory trying to recall where she knew him from, when her father looked up. "Ruthie, meet your mother-in-law!"

Ruth fainted.

Ruth's mom was on the verge of splitting apart at the seams, she was so stressed. She had been fussing and fretting all day.

"Ruthie, you look like a princess," she said, and then she burst into tears, buried her face in her apron and for at least the tenth time that day moaned, "You're just a baby! How can my baby be getting married? It just seems like yesterday you were crawling around the floor a chubby, naked . . ."

"Mom!" Ruth snipped. *"Please!"* They were both surprised by a loud commotion outside the tent.

"Oh my, they're here!"

It seemed like everyone from the community had shown up to escort Ruth from her parents' tent to her new home. They were singing, laughing and twirling their lamps as the flames danced in the clear night air. As they approached, the groom stepped out of his tent. He looked as nervous as she felt. He was a year or two older than Ruth, perhaps fifteen or sixteen, she thought. His family had moved here from Israel a few years ago just after the famine had begun. The two of them stood shyly grinning at each other as the people danced and shouted. He whispered something into her ear; she shivered with delight at his deep, husky, exotic accent. As the music paused, Ruth's father gently removed her veil, placed it on the groom's shoulder and said, "The government shall be on his shoulders."

With that a man sprang out behind them, startling the young couple. He was holding what must have been the biggest saber known to man. It flashed brilliantly in the clear moonlit night; the reflection of the fiery torches sparkled red and orange. Suddenly, the man wielded it above his head, twirled it once and brought it swooshing down, severing a pomegranate—which sat on the doorstep of the tent—clean in half. *Boom!* The drum exploded back into its driving rhythm as people cheered, "May the grains of this fruit symbolize your many offspring!"

Ruth fainted.

The first couple of years of marriage seemed to fly by. It took a while for Ruth to get used to her new home and family, but she really grew to love them. She loved sitting in the shade outside the tent with her mother-in-law, Naomi, sewing, preparing food and listening to stories about her home and the God of Israel. Yahweh seemed so different from the gods of Moab. Ruth had always feared the fickle Baal of Peor, who seemed unpredictable and uninterested. Naomi's God was holy and pure, yet approachable and loving. It didn't take long for him to win Ruth's heart and devotion.

The recession seemed only to get worse. People prophesied its end and the coming good times, but evidently the recession didn't get the message. As foreigners, Naomi's family struggled to pick up odd jobs. Sometimes the ends just didn't meet. Then, when it seemed like things couldn't get any worse . . . they did. An epidemic, probably carried from a distant country by one of the traveling merchants, broke out. Ruth's husband and brother-in-law both became ill. It seemed that the whole country was grieving over lost loved ones. Some families lost just an aunt or a distant cousin; others lost brothers, sisters, parents, wives and grandchildren. Ruthie lost her husband.

Times were tough; they were even tougher for three widows. (Naomi's husband had also died.) Naomi couldn't sleep at night. She would pace around outside, collapse on the ground in a heap and bury her head in her lap, crying. Then she would start all over again. She was a foreigner far from her relatives with no one to help. Was there any hope at all? Slowly the dark clouds of despair began to recede, just a little. A passing caravan brought news that the famine had ended in Israel. It was time to go home. It had been almost ten years since Naomi had seen her homeland. She had left with a husband and two fine sons. She would return empty.

"Ruthie, you're breaking my heart! I love you as if you were my own, but you should stay here. Stay with your people. Orpah is staying. She

already has her eye on a young man. What hope is there for you with me? You're young, and beautiful . . . you will find another husband. You're breaking my heart," Naomi repeated over and over as the tears streamed down her tanned face. Ruth held Naomi's face and gently rubbed the tears aside with her thumbs.

Don't urge me to leave you or to turn back from you. Where you go I will go, and where you stay I will stay. Your people will be my people and your God my God. . . . May the LORD deal with me, be it ever so severely, if anything but death separates you and me. **Ruth 1:16, 17**

Ruth embraced a lifestyle of holiness that hurts the eyes. She was not going to be squeezed back into the world's mold by the circumstances. She was not going to mindlessly obey the dictates of her culture or generation in a desperate attempt to fit in and find acceptance. She determined to have an attitude of righteousness and holiness, to be countercultural.

How Do We Develop a Lifestyle of Holiness Like Ruth Did?

When I was at school, my friends would meet me at the park every evening to play soccer. Although we were anxious to get started, we still had to spend at least the first five minutes arguing over who would "be" the superstar player we all idolized. You know how it goes—everyone has their favorite player whom they want to be in the game. "I'm Shaq . . . well I'm LeBron!" On it goes. We all spent hours watching our favorite players. We studied their moves, the way they celebrated a great play—we even knew what type of deodorant and underwear they wore.

When the game finally got underway, we would try our best to imitate

the slick moves of our idols. We acknowledged the fans, just as they did. We imitated their rituals, copied their characteristic stance and mimicked their moves. Whenever we scored we would celebrate in their trademark fashion. We even had the all-important underwear on. But did we play like the great one? No. Despite the fact that we knew the wave, how to stick out our tongue and all about the secret underwear, we just didn't seem to be able to dominate as they did. Why, you ask?

The answer is simple. Our heroes did not become great athletes just by learning how to respond in a certain way during the game. Sorry, but the underwear is not the key to greatness. Tiger Woods is not Tiger because he learned how to pump his fist after a great shot, how to characteristically shuffle his feet before an important putt or what brand of clothing to wear. Our heroes are great because of a lifestyle of discipline. They have dedicated their lives to training and preparation. They sacrifice sleep to get up early and train. When everyone else has gone home, they are still practicing or working on areas to improve. When their friends are chillin' at the mall, they are practicing shots over and over or running miles to get in top condition. It is a lifestyle of preparation of mind and body to provide a foundation for their responses in the game. We cannot hope to be like the great ones just by copying their moves during a game, because that is not how they became great.

Jesus has called us all to live holy lives. *Holy* means "to be set apart for God." As Christians we are to be set apart from the actions of the world and live lives of purity dedicated to him, just as a great athlete rises above and is set apart from the others. But we will not be able to respond in purity in any situation if we do not have the lifestyle foundation. If we live our lives trying to be as much like the world as possible while remaining Christians, we will fail when we find ourselves in tense situations. When we feel the press and warmth of another's body and our hormones are pumping, will we have the lifestyle of preparation to respond in purity? When every-

one else is edging us to swallow the pill and dance all night or to go to an inappropriate movie, how will we handle it? Are we willing to be different, or is it just easier to be like everyone else?

Ruth had developed a lifestyle that was set apart for God and his principles. She was not just going to follow the way of the world and be pressured by it. She knew that none of her friends were happy and fulfilled anyway. She looked at the faces of the people as they came out of the temple after an all-night rave. They looked emptier than when they went in. She could almost see the huge gaping holes in their souls, dying to be filled, aching for something that always seemed to be beyond their grasp. Their faces were fragile masks, trying to keep up the illusion of fulfillment while struggling with depression and a deep longing for the final "rest" promised by suicide.

Flee

The first step in a lifestyle of holiness is in . . . the opposite direction! Everything in Ruth wanted to follow Naomi's advice to go back to her culture and lifestyle. It would have been easier and more comfortable just to go with the flow. But when Naomi encouraged her to give in to the temptation, Ruth took a big step away.

Run from anything that stimulates youthful lust. Follow anything that makes you want to do right. Pursue faith and love and peace, and enjoy the companionship of those who call on the Lord with pure hearts.
2 Timothy 2:22, NLT

A wise pursuer of God doesn't seek temptation. Ruth made wise decisions to stay away from situations that could tempt her to sin. It is much harder to resist temptation when it's right in front of you and your peers are

telling you that it's OK and that everyone does it. Let's be honest—it's not realistic to think that we can just stick our heads in the ground and avoid exposure to everything around us. It's impossible. But be wise. Choose what you do, where you go, what you read or what you watch—carefully. Ask yourself, "Is this building my relationship with Jesus?"

Try to live in peace with everyone, and seek to live a clean and holy life, for those who are not holy will not see the Lord. **Hebrews 12:14,** NLT

We must take responsibility for our actions and choices. Don't give yourself a guilt trip or beat yourself up over every decision; just be thoughtful. Be ready to go against the flow and make your stand for holiness. Ruth knew the best way to avoid tripping was to stay away from the potholes.

The small bustling town of Bethlehem was so different from the desert tents of Ruth's home. The town spread lazily over a hillside with the small adobe houses tumbling down each side to the valley below, where the tall barley stalks swayed gently in the afternoon breeze. Ruth paused under a fig tree as the breeze playfully danced on her face. It had been a long journey, but Ruth was out of bed before the sun the next morning.

"Child, what are you doing making all that noise at this time of day?" Naomi asked, somewhat quizzical, somewhat annoyed.

"I thought I would go glean in the harvest fields," replied Ruth light-heartedly, as she slipped on her sandals.

Now, if truth be told, Ruth had put on her brave face for Naomi because she didn't want her to worry, but she was quite nervous about going to the fields. What if the owner of the field wasn't friendly? Surely he would realize she was a foreigner, and a Moabite at that. Tensions were high between the two nations; would anyone welcome her? Her heart was pounding and

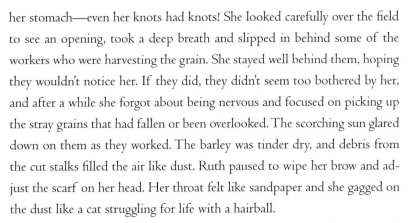

her stomach—even her knots had knots! She looked carefully over the field to see an opening, took a deep breath and slipped in behind some of the workers who were harvesting the grain. She stayed well behind them, hoping they wouldn't notice her. If they did, they didn't seem too bothered by her, and after a while she forgot about being nervous and focused on picking up the stray grains that had fallen or been overlooked. The scorching sun glared down on them as they worked. The barley was tinder dry, and debris from the cut stalks filled the air like dust. Ruth paused to wipe her brow and adjust the scarf on her head. Her throat felt like sandpaper and she gagged on the dust like a cat struggling for life with a hairball.

They worked in the fields from sunup till sundown. By the time Ruth got home, all she wanted to do was collapse in her bed and go to sleep. Naomi's jaw almost hit the ground when the five-gallon bag of grain thumped to the ground.

"Did you rob a bank? Where on earth did all that come from? Take it back before we get into trouble."

"Mom!" said Ruth, snapping a little in her fatigue. Then, energized by the realization that she had just single-handedly set the gleaning world record, Ruth recounted the day.

"Boaz!" Naomi exclaimed, as Ruth told her whose field she had been working in.

"I always said he would grow up to be a fine young man. You know, I remember when he was just a boy. He would catch locusts and pull their back legs off. Your auntie-in-law thought he was going to grow up to be a hooligan. 'Mark my words,' I used to say, 'mark my words, that young Boaz will grow up to be a fine young man one day . . .'"

Naomi was about to get seriously into the flow of reminiscing when she interrupted herself, "Is he married?" Then without drawing breath (as all moms do who seem to be able to speak endlessly, fueled by some supernatural gift of oxygen), she flew into a discourse extolling Boaz's manhood.

"Mother!" Ruth turned as red with embarrassment as a vine-ripe tomato. The truth was, her heart had fluttered when she saw Boaz. She had been trying to convince herself all afternoon that it was the heat that made her giddy when Boaz spoke to her, but she wasn't buying it.

The next evening when Ruth returned from the fields, Naomi was ready and waiting. Her face betrayed her excitement. She beamed like a twelve-year-old who had just been told the world's biggest secret. Ruth's curiosity finally got the better of her.

"You know you want to tell me . . . so come on, out with it."

Naomi giggled like a schoolgirl as she told Ruth her news.

"A kinsman *what?*" Ruth questioned.

"Redeemer," said Naomi. "If a man dies without children, we have a custom called the levirate, which calls the next of kin to marry the widow and give offspring. Boaz is your next of kin. Now, here is the plan . . ."

"You look like a princess," Naomi muttered as she hugged Ruthie tight, burying her face on her shoulder as she wept. Ruth thought of her own mom on the night of her wedding. It seemed like a lifetime away. She had been through so much since then, but God had been faithful. The dusk was drawing in as Ruth walked down the hill toward the fields she had been working in all week. She felt very anxious. Quietly, she tiptoed up to the campfire where Boaz and the workers were asleep, guarding the grain. She could feel her heart pounding in her throat as she tentatively raised a corner of the blanket covering Boaz. She was afraid to breathe as she lifted the covering from his feet, exposing them to the night chill. Without any warning, Boaz, still half-asleep, rolled toward her as she knelt next to him and in a sleepy haze threw his arm around her waist. Ruth froze. She was petrified that he was awake and had caught her. She waited in motionless agony for what seemed like an eternity. Slowly she began to shift away letting Boaz's arm fall, ever so gently, to the ground beside him. Ruth was in agony. For a moment she longed just to slide in next to Boaz and feel his strong arm

around her waist and snuggle into his chest. He smelled so good. She ached to feel his gentle breath on her face.

Snap out of it, girlfriend! she commanded herself.

At last she was free. Boaz slept on. She quietly crawled over to the fire and curled up by his feet. She lay there, looking up at the stars, playing every possible scenario over and over in her head. She was just drifting asleep when Boaz suddenly sat straight up.

"What the . . . ?"

He looked at his chilly feet and then at Ruth. Her face glowed like an angel's in the night fire.

"God bless you, Ruthie. You have not run after the young men, whether rich or poor. You have acted with purity and integrity. Everyone knows you are a woman of noble character." As the flames glowed and flickered, lapping the late night air, Boaz asked Ruthie to marry him.

Pursue

Pursue righteousness, faith, love and peace. 2 Timothy 2:22

Stepping away was only half the task.

1. Ruth Pursued Righteousness.

Not having a righteousness of my own that comes from the law, but that which is through faith in Christ—the righteousness that comes from God and is by faith. Philippians 3:9

Righteousness is not something we do. It is a position. We are made "right with God" in our relationship with Jesus. Ruth pursued a deep, living, vibrant relationship with her heavenly Father.

2. Ruth Pursued Faith.

How can a young person stay pure? By obeying your word and following its rules. **Psalm 119:9,** NLT

Ruth buried God's Word deep inside so it was ready when she needed to draw on it, just like an athlete practices the same move over and over so that during the game it's effortless. Let the Word of God renew your mind and your view of yourself. Ruth knew these truths and they shaped her perceptions. You are forgiven (Ephesians 4:32), righteous (Philippians 3:9), perfect (Colossians 1:28), a new creation (2 Corinthians 5:17), sanctified and holy (1 Corinthians 1:2), free from condemnation (Romans 8:1), dead to sin but alive to God (Romans 6:11), given incomparably great power (Ephesians 1:19), filled with the mind of Christ (1 Corinthians 2:16), holy and without blame (1 Peter 1:16), more than conquerors (Romans 8:37) and loved (1 John 3:16). This is your true identity. Be who you are—everything else is an illusion.

3. Ruth Pursued Love.

Real love respects and cares for others. Real love never says, "If you love me you will do this . . ." Pushing someone to compromise isn't real love; it's love of self. Remember whose property you are touching—that person belongs to Jesus. In a way, he or she *is* Jesus!

The King will reply, "I tell you the truth, whatever you did for one of the least of these . . . you did for me." **Matthew 25:40**

Real love cares for the heart. Real love is a commitment to the other person's best interests.

4. Ruth Pursued Peace.

She acknowledged the presence of God in every activity. Nothing she did was outside of God's presence.

Pray that you will not fall into temptation. **Luke 22:40**

How long do you spend preparing to go on a date? Do you spend as much time praying for God's guidance for that time?

Along with those who call on the Lord out of a pure heart.

2 Timothy 2:22

Ruth surrounded herself with people who stirred up her passion for God. The number one reason people don't embrace Christianity is that they don't see any difference between a Christian and themselves. What about us—do our lives look different? Could the people in our school, workplace or community tell the difference? How does our faith influence our behavior? Our lives should be above reproach or blame. Our actions, not our words, show people what really impacts our lives. We may talk about Christianity, but do our lives back up our words? Do we walk in integrity and purity? St. Francis of Assisi said, "Preach the gospel at all times. If necessary, use words." If we watch inappropriate movies, go too far on a date or tell a "little white lie," what are we saying to the world that watches us?

Don't let anyone look down on you because you are young, but set an example for the believers in speech, in life, in love, in faith and in purity.
1 Timothy 4:12

Our lives must be examples that lead others to full devotion in Christ. If you feel you are young and insignificant, think again. God has a plan for your life and will use your radical commitment to holiness just as he did Ruth's. Just like her, you're special to God, overflowing with gifting, calling, ability and destiny; he has a call on your life to rewrite history through your holiness. God has a huge, crazy dream for your life; you will impact the history of this world like no other generation before you. Lead the way, set the example.

A single life committed to holiness can have incredible cosmic impact. Our devotion to holiness doesn't just affect us; it is a partnership with the creator in the "great reversal"—the redemption of creation. Our commitment to holiness creates a heritage that others will build upon. Marrying Boaz wasn't the end of Ruth's story. They had a son named Obed. Obed was the father of Jesse, and Jesse the father of David. David became the king of Israel, a man after God's heart. He reaped the heritage of his great-grandmother, a woman with holiness that hurt the eyes, a foreigner from Moab called Ruth. If that were the entire story, it would still be pretty awesome, but it's not. There's more. Many years later in the same bustling town of Bethlehem, a direct descendant of David was born. His name was Jesus. Guess who his great- (times twenty-nine!) grandmother was? You've guessed it—Ruth. Jesus reaped the heritage of a young woman with holiness that hurts the eyes.

Making Waves

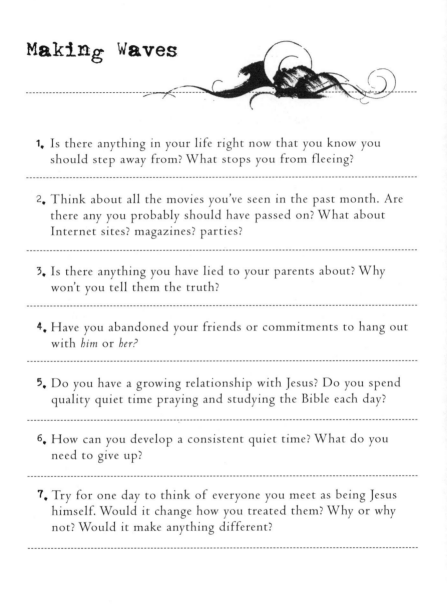

1. Is there anything in your life right now that you know you should step away from? What stops you from fleeing?

---

2. Think about all the movies you've seen in the past month. Are there any you probably should have passed on? What about Internet sites? magazines? parties?

---

3. Is there anything you have lied to your parents about? Why won't you tell them the truth?

---

4. Have you abandoned your friends or commitments to hang out with *him* or *her?*

---

5. Do you have a growing relationship with Jesus? Do you spend quality quiet time praying and studying the Bible each day?

---

6. How can you develop a consistent quiet time? What do you need to give up?

---

7. Try for one day to think of everyone you meet as being Jesus himself. Would it change how you treated them? Why or why not? Would it make anything different?

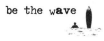

List three things God has shown you in this chapter that you don't want to forget.

1.
_____

_____

2.
_____

_____

3.
_____

_____

Be the Wave

Lord, from this moment on I commit to . . .

Spend a few minutes talking to God about how you feel. List some specific prayer points that will help you live out the truths in this chapter.

_____

_____

_____

_____

_____

_____

_____

_____

facing your Goliaths

David

Jay slumped down in the chair. A creaky, old ceiling fan groaned as it fought rust and years of dust in a struggle to turn. He stared at the screen reading his e-mail.

Thailand? How am I supposed to get to Thailand? I don't even have enough money for food; there's no way I can go to Thailand!

He felt a fog of silent despair engulf him. Jay, just 22, had recently left friends, family, everything he knew and followed the call of God to China. Things had been going well but not without challenges. Money was very tight, and even when he had enough to go shopping, he didn't know what to buy because he couldn't read the labels. He struggled to find any word he recognized on the packaging; his Chinese was almost nonexistent.

God, what do I do? It would be great to go to Thailand and see other missionaries—anyone who speaks English—but how?

Thailand was just a few hours away on a plane, but it could have been the ends of the earth to Jay. As he sat dejectedly staring at the e-mail, he had a strange thought:

You will go to Thailand.

The next few days were a roller coaster of emotions as his faith ebbed and flowed. He had a growing sense in his spirit that he should go to Thailand, but where was the money? He prayed, "Lord, I feel it is your will to go, but how?"

Silently he waited for God to speak. Then the oddest idea came to mind. He felt God was saying to go as far as he could. *But that would just be to*

the airport, Lord . . . are you sure about this?

He began to wonder if this idea was really God's at all. Finally, the day came. He would have to fly today or forget the whole thing. He struggled to stop his stomach churning with nerves as he rode the bus to the airport. This had to be the craziest thing he had ever done. With every passing minute fear and doubt grew. *This is just dumb. How can anything happen? No one even knows I'm going to the airport!*

He slowly walked into the terminal and approached the airline counter. Good, they still had a seat available . . . for what that was worth. The plane would leave in just a few hours, but he was still no closer to getting on it. He sat on a bench opposite the ticket counter. *OK, Lord, this is as far as I can go.*

An hour passed, then another, and another. Jay looked at the clock. The plane would board soon, and he would have to make the long bus ride home. His situation was impossible. He was staring at a full-sized Goliath (straight in the belly button). His last glimmer of faith began to ebb away.

Just then a Japanese man sat next to him and said, "Hello. You don't see too many Westerners in this airport. What are you doing here?"

Jay almost forgot to reply as he stared at this man speaking perfect English. He felt a bit silly as he sheepishly told the man why he was sitting in the middle of an airport in western China. He stammered as he quickly finished his embarrassing tale. Without a word the man pulled his wallet out of his pocket, emptied its contents and gave it all to Jay. "Here, go get on your plane."

Minutes later Jay was sitting on the plane, looking out the small oval window as the airport grew smaller and smaller beneath him.

Have you ever come face-to-face with a Goliath? It can be anything. A relationship, money, a problem at school or at home . . . anything. It appears out of nowhere. Its intimidating size drains us of hope; the enormous difficulty that casts a shadow of gloom over our future leaves us feeling beaten. Chances are, you're staring a Goliath in the face right now.

David was a teenager when he came face-to-face with a problem called Goliath. The infant nation of Israel assembled for battle against the powerful Philistines at the valley of Elah. The Philistines were a warring nation. It was their national industry, so to speak. Their expert blacksmiths (I Samuel 13:19) developed technology and skills to make impressive weapons and armor for battle. Every soldier was arrayed from head to toe in a uniform of expertly crafted bronze armor (I Samuel 17:5-7). Each wore a bronze helmet with great plumes of feathers erupting from the top. The vivid, frightening plume made the wearer appear almost two feet taller than he really was. Their heavy, impenetrable chest plates were brightly polished and gleamed in the sunlight. Their arms and legs were clad in sturdy leather and bronze. Each soldier was rigorously trained and prepared for combat. They were armed to the teeth with swords, spears and shields. A terrifying sight, they looked like ancient metallic terminators. Nothing seemed to penetrate this unstoppable nightmare.

Israel didn't even have a national army. It was not until King Solomon's reign about 90 years later that a national armed force was developed. Up to this point, Israel was still just a loose confederation of farmers; they were not even a proper nation yet. Their only bond was tribal, extending back to twelve brothers who didn't even seem to get along with each other. When Israel needed to protect itself, an appeal would go out through all the territories, and men would gather at a designated town. The guys would literally come straight from their fields. They would grab a pitchfork, a goad (a sort of cattle prod), an axe or a rock for a weapon. They had no armor, only the simple clothes they wore every day. They couldn't even make the most basic sword. Only two people in the whole country owned a sword or armor, the king and the prince. They were genuine country bumpkins, complete with sandals and pitchforks, chewing pieces of hay.

The Philistine army, arrayed in full battle armor, assembled for battle

along the western ridge of the valley. This was strategic. The rising eastern sun would glare on their polished bronze uniforms, creating a terrifying vision. The tall Philistines appeared like monsters two feet taller than they were. The dazzling sunlight glared off their armor, making it almost impossible to look at them. Any enemy melted with fear at the sight of this monstrous, metallic army. They were awesome, equipped, trained, snarling and armed to the teeth. Opposite them stood a straggling bunch of hillbilly farmers holding sticks and stones.

Israel was outnumbered, outgunned and outmatched. The mighty Philistine army could have rolled over their prey, squashing them like an insignificant bug. Instead, they chose to send one man to fight for them— winner takes all. It was risky to gamble their obvious advantage on the prowess of one man. They could have used their sheer force and superiority to pummel the Israelites with ease. But they were so confident of victory and looked down at Israel with such disdain that they didn't even want to get their uniforms dirty. Why break a sweat, or a nail, against this bunch of low-life rabble? It wasn't worth the energy. So the Philistines picked their champion (1 Samuel 17:4) for the ultimate face-off.

Now, when it comes to picking one person to represent the fate of an entire nation, you really want to send the best you've got—the one you're most confident will win. It's like the Olympic Games. We scour the nation to make sure we have the absolute fastest, strongest and quickest. We spend millions to be sure we've found those who have the best chance of success. Most started training for that moment when they were six or seven years old. Year after year, they discipline themselves to get up early in the morning and train for hours each day. While others are enjoying themselves or going out to parties, they go to bed early, watch what they eat, or put in extra time at the gym. That is the sort of determination, discipline and training it takes to be the best. We spend huge amounts of time and money for a ten-second sprint or a lap in the pool—how much more if our entire

nation's freedom were on the line? What if the second-place prize was a lifetime of slavery?

The Israelites shook in their sandals when they got a close-up of the raw power of Goliath. He was immense. Goliath stood a towering nine feet tall (I Samuel 17:4). The average Israeli was around five-foot-nothing. With his helmet and battle armor Goliath loomed over them—almost twice their size. The shaft of his spear looked like a telephone pole. His powerful sword would crush and shatter bones with a single flick of his wrist. His shield looked more like the roof of a house that had been mercilessly ripped off and strapped to his bulging arm. The men of Israel, straight from the farm, quivered like weak stalks of grain during a gale-force wind. There they stood before a mountain of a man, their knees knocking in abject fear.

Goliath bellowed his challenge, sneering at the Israelites. He must have been laughing. He was nine feet tall, apparently nine feet wide and as strong as an ox, laden with weapons of annihilation, with the sun glaring off his armor and blinding his prey. He had been trained and prepared since his youth for this arena, and he was ready. Just that morning he'd had a case of Mountain Dew® and he was fired up. His heart was thumping. The veins on his forehead were pumping purple with rage. He was like a wild beast that had just broken loose from his cage. Goliath was manic; pain was on his mind. He wanted to rip someone's head off. And who was his mighty and worthy opponent? A five-foot scrawny farmer with a rock? This isn't a battle; it's a joke. Daily Goliath stomped over and bellowed his degrading slander. Was there anyone who would be a real man and fight for honor?

No! The Bible says they were "dismayed" and "afraid." They fell to the ground horrified, as if all strength and will to live had left them. It was definitely their worst nightmare. Twice a day, day after day, Goliath challenged them, and twice a day, for forty days, no one dared to move. They cowered on the floor in fear. Didn't they look at each other helplessly and wonder how long they could go on? Perhaps they did, but no one was

bothered enough to risk his neck trying to change the situation. So twice a day Goliath, with venomous disdain, walked over to the Israelites and taunted his enemy. Peering down into the trenches, Goliath tried to goad them into action, spitting on them and demeaning them. He humiliated and scorned them as he cursed them with his foul words of contempt. Each man buried his face in the dirt floor of the trench, scared stiff and afraid to make eye contact. The situation was hopeless.

But wait a minute—these were God's chosen people. The people who saw the mighty walls of Jericho fall with just a shout to God. Where was God now? He was right there, but they had stopped looking to him and were looking to themselves for deliverance. They saw themselves as unable to go into battle, for the enemy was too great for *them*. They saw themselves as five-foot tall, scrawny farmers, unarmed and without a chance. In the shadow of Goliath, they forgot the promises of God and focused on how they could fix the problem themselves.

While Israel was still trudging around the desert with Moses, God had shown them how to face their Goliaths. According to God's instructions in Deuteronomy 20, once everyone had assembled for battle, the priest was to approach the men and encourage them not to be fainthearted. God was the one who would fight against their enemies to save them (Deuteronomy 20:3, 4). The priest would remind the men that they were covenant partners of the almighty God; they had omnipotent power in their corner. Then, the captain of the army would walk to the front of the assembly, face the men and say something like, "Good morning, chaps. I have our battle briefing here, but before I begin . . . has anyone built a new house and not dedicated it?" (Deuteronomy 20:5).

The men would look at one another in confusion. *Shouldn't he be talking about the battle strategy? Why is he talking about real estate?* Slowly, those who had recently become homeowners would raise their hands in acknowledgment.

Then the captain would break into the baffled murmuring, "OK, why don't you guys go home and take care of that!"

Wait a minute! This is ridiculous. You do not send troops home when you are about to face a great enemy; at times like these you need every man available. Everyone knows the idea is to overpower the enemy with numbers and firepower. Still the captain continued, "Has anyone planted a vineyard and not begun to enjoy it?" (Deuteronomy 20:6).

Now what? Why is he asking about farming at a time like this? Of course, many hands would be raised. This was a nation of farmers. Again the captain released them to go home and prepare the wine for the victory celebration. This was insane! Those who were left began to panic. Surely this captain was a sandwich short of a full picnic. The throng of fighting men was really beginning to thin out. What was going on? They would be like lambs led to the slaughter!

By the time the third question was asked, the captain's leadership skills were seriously being questioned. "Has anyone become pledged to a woman and not married her?" (Deuteronomy 20:7).

Most of the brave young men fell into this category. All of the young guys with the energy and adrenaline to be extreme and radical raised their hands. "Well, off you go as well. Enjoy the wedding. Save us a piece of cake!" replied the captain.

The ranks were now severely depleted. The strong builders and farmers—men in their prime—were all gone. The zealous young guys were out of sight, leaving a motley bunch of flabby, good old boys. There were large gaps between each remaining man where their fellow soldiers had once stood. They no longer felt like a force to be reckoned with. In fact, they felt a bit isolated. Each man slowly shuffled toward his neighbor for support, but there was still one more order of business. The captain looked serious and stern as he asked, "Is any man afraid or fainthearted?" (Deuteronomy 20:8).

After this fiasco—you bet! Many hands shot up into the air. All the men

had assembled for what was to be a difficult and hard-fought war. They would need all hands on deck, but this captain had sent everyone home. Of course they were afraid. The captain suddenly took on a defiant look. His eye twinkled with confidence and courage as he simply and calmly said, "You can go as well because you make your brothers nervous!" (Deuteronomy 20:8).

The battle was the Lord's.

> *For the Lord your God is the one who goes with you to fight for you against your enemies to give you victory.* **Deuteronomy 20:4**

Their fight was God's fight—the Lord was responsible for the outcome. All God needed was one man to stand for him in trusting obedience, and any man at that, for the battle was his. He was Israel's champion. If a nation challenged Israel, they challenged God. Numbers, size, strength, the physical—all that man would look at for fighting—especially as a representative warrior, was not important. In fact, the Lord did not want too many men in case the people became proud and thought too much of themselves. (Judges 7:2). Judges 7 tells us of an army led by Gideon. When they assembled, they went through the principles of Deuteronomy 20, but there were too many left behind. God didn't want too many men. If he gave them the victory, they might think they had had something to do with it. So off they went for a drink of water, and God weeded out more of them on the basis of their drinking style! When we face our Goliaths, we are not alone because the battle is the Lord's.

When Israel came and stood at the valley of Elah, they had forgotten God's promise. No one stepped forward and declared that the battle was the Lord's. After forty days, a teenager showed up to check out the battle.

He was not old enough to go to war. His job was to watch the sheep and stand them back up when they tipped over. But he loved God and lived his life in obedient trust.

As David arrived he walked along the battle line, eagerly looking to see how the fight was going. After all, it had been forty days—it would have to be a great crusade to last so long. He found his brothers and caught up on all the news over the cheese sandwiches he brought. While they were speaking, up came Goliath. David was thrilled and he pricked up his ears. He could feel the electricity in the air. Goliath, insolent as ever, arrogantly challenged David's brothers and countrymen. David's heart began to race and thump in his chest. The hairs on the back of his neck stood up like knives. He knew that any minute now these guys were going to break into a rowdy chorus of "Did You Feel the Mountains Tremble?" and charge for Goliath! David stood there transfixed, his eyes and mouth wide open. Then slowly he looked around. What were his brothers doing on the ground? Had someone lost a contact?

David couldn't believe his eyes. "Who is this uncircumcised Philistine that he should defy the armies of the living God?" he demanded (I Samuel 17:26).

Circumcision was the sign of God's covenant promise never to leave or forsake his chosen people, always to fight for them. David looked unbelievingly at his brothers.

"Hey, guys, doesn't he realize who we are? What a fool! He doesn't know anything about our faithful God."

But his brothers were with the rest of the people, eating dirt. They became upset and angry with David. Most of us get angry and defensive when we know we are wrong and are embarrassed, don't we? David's brother retorted,

Why have you come down here? And with whom did you leave those few sheep in the desert? I know how conceited you are and how wicked your heart is; you came down only to watch the battle. **1 Samuel 17:28**

Ouch! That's a harsh response to your kid brother. Poor David was bewildered, "Now what have I done?" (v. 29). He wasn't being childish. This wasn't the remark of a silly young kid who didn't know what life in the real world was like. David knew very well. Not many of us have been left by ourselves all night to wrestle with lions and bears that are trying to help themselves to a snack at an all-you-can-eat lamb buffet. Imagine a kid in his early teens having to camp out by himself all night and deal with wild lions and bears. During those times, when his knees were knocking and he trembled with fear as a ferocious bear stood up on its back legs and roared with rage, David had learned to depend on God. He discovered that it didn't matter if he was young and inexperienced. God was in his corner.

So many of the grown-ups were embarrassed by David's protest, he was hauled before the king. King Saul was a big, muscular guy—he stood head and shoulders above anyone in Israel (1 Samuel 10:23). If anyone should have taken Goliath's challenge and been a man, it was the leader. But Saul wasn't about to put his life on the line. Even he was so focused on the size of the problem that he forgot God. Saul's conversation with Dave must have been one of the weirdest in history. There was the king, a big, muscular, grown man, letting a scrawny teenager fight when his nation's future was on the line. No doubt Saul had already conceded defeat. He was beaten before he left his tent. *Someone is going to have to die. If this kid wants to be the crazy one, he can go for it.*

Saul asked David, "He's a tough fella, that Goliath. This is going to be a hard battle; have you had *any* experience?"

Your servant has killed both the lion and the bear; this uncircumcised
Philistine will be like one of them, because he has defied the armies of
the living God. **1 Samuel 17:36**

Saul, being a nice guy, and probably feeling a bit guilty about sending David out to be slaughtered, tried to help him as best he could. He gave him a quick fencing lesson and offered David the bit of armor he had. It didn't fit David. Each generation has to stand for itself before God. It has to have the freedom to experience, worship and follow God in the way it feels most comfortable. Too often, older generations try to force the younger to look, dress and act like them. But it doesn't fit. You have to find your own relationship, your own expression, with God. Our Father doesn't care about outward appearances, clothes or styles of worship; David proved that. God is looking for those who will abandon all to worship him with their whole heart, in spirit and in truth. The Lord loves you, believes in you and will always be right there with you. He accepts you the way you are. Express God's overwhelming love in your life your way . . . he loves that stuff!

I have to be honest with you; I wish I could have the kind of confidence David showed. He boldly proclaimed, "I'm going to strike you down, and not just you, Goliath, but your nation as well" (vv. 45, 46).

How could he be so sure? He knew the battle was the Lord's (v. 47). It had nothing to do with him. David was so confident he ran toward Goliath (v. 48).

Goliath's blood was boiling. What an insult—sending a child to fight him! He was going to pull David's arms off and beat him with them! David laughed, "You don't get it, do you? You haven't read the rule book. You're not fighting a boy, you're up against almighty God!"

Goliath was so furious he lost his head.

So How Do We Face Our Goliaths?

1. Step Back

The first thing to do when a Goliath jumps in front of you is to take a step back and gain perspective. Take a small object, like a coin, and put it right in front of your face. What can you see? A coin, nothing more; but put the coin down on the floor and you can see clearly. The coin doesn't look so big anymore. With a change of position comes a change of perspective. Sometimes when we are struggling through things in our daily lives, they seem huge. They block our path and are all we can see. God has a different perspective. To him it's not so big. When a problem rears up that seems insurmountable, take a step back, and get God's perspective. When David came to the camp, all the men were focused on the problem and had lost their focus. Goliath seemed so big it was all they could see. David stepped back, focused on God and got a new perspective.

2. Trust God's Faithfulness

Next, remember God's faithfulness in the past. God has a pretty good track record. David reminded Saul, "Yep, my job is to put the sheep back up when they tip over . . . the bears and lions are up to God."

David focused on God's proven character, and trusted him. To trust God in faith is not the blind leap many think it is. Have you ever ordered something from a magazine, the TV or the Internet? What do you begin to do after a few days? You start to watch for the mailman, anticipating the arrival of your package. Now that is blind faith. If we can trust people that we have never met before, when we have no previous history with them, and whom we have never even seen, why don't we have more faith in God? His track record is proven. Before we even cared, he gave up the universe to come down here and demonstrate his love and faithfulness to us.

If we are faithless, he will remain faithful, for he cannot disown himself.
2 Timothy 2:13

Never will I leave you; never will I forsake you. **Hebrews 13:5**

Be strong and courageous. Do not be afraid or terrified because of them, for the LORD your God goes with you; he will never leave you nor forsake you. **Deuteronomy 31:6**

No one in Israel's camp responded to Goliath—for forty days and nights—because no one wanted to fail. If we refuse to face our Goliaths and never attempt anything, we will never fail at anything. We can timidly shuffle through life with our heads down, pretending that Goliath isn't there. We can think up thousands of great reasons to justify not stepping out in faith, and we will never fail. But it will be a boring, timid existence of holding back. We can trust God.

3. *Know His Promises*

Here's the next thing. God has promised to always be with us, but if we don't know his promises, how will we be able to trust him? We have to know his Word. If we try to live off someone else's relationship with God or knowledge of the Bible—we are in trouble. We can't rely on our friend, parent or pastor. We have to know God's promises for ourselves. That means reading his Word and remembering it, so it's there when we need it. Remember when Jesus was in the wilderness and the devil came to tempt him? Jesus responded each time by quoting the Bible. We have to know his Word to overcome our doubt and fears.

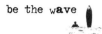

How can a young man keep his way pure? By living according to your word. . . .
I have hidden your word in my heart that I might not sin against you.

Psalm 119:9, 11

When David faced Goliath he knew God's promises.

4. *Work on Your Walk*

Fourthly, walk with God before Goliath shows up. The time to start looking for God's promises, or trying to cultivate a relationship with him, is not when Goliath is standing in front of you. Develop your relationship with God now, not when the chips are down. Does that mean we can't look for promises and seek God when Goliath is in front of us? No. But, it's not the best time for introductions. Saul offered David some cool, shiny armor, but David already had his own.

5. *Remember That the Battle Is the Lord's*

Finally, remember that the battle is the Lord's. If we are following Jesus in obedience, it is his problem, not ours. We become anxious when we think the problem is ours to solve. We stay up at night worrying what to do, trying to figure it all out. Jesus said that all our worrying couldn't even add a single moment to our lives. Leave that to him. Paul told the believers in Philippi,

Don't fret or worry. Instead of worrying, pray. Let petitions and praises shape your worries into prayers, letting God know your concerns. Before you know it, a sense of God's wholeness, everything coming together for

good, will come and settle you down. It's wonderful what happens when Christ displaces worry at the center of your life.

Philippians 4:6, 7, The Message

It's not about our strength or our ability. It doesn't matter how many battles we've been in. It's all about him. Our Father has promised that he will always be there for us; it's his sworn duty. That Goliath isn't too big for God—trust him. His character is proven. He loves you unconditionally. His promises will never fail. The battle is the Lord's.

Making Waves

---

1. Think about the last problem you had. How did you handle it? Was it effective? Why or why not?

---

2. If "Goliath" showed up today, where would your relationship with God be? What can you do to improve the foundation?

---

3. Reread Philippians 4:6. What are some practical ways you can stop being anxious and give your problems to God?

---

4. Do you have a regular time to read the Bible? Will you commit to one?

---

5. Do you memorize God's promises? Will you begin to do that regularly?

---

6. Do you have a "Goliath" in your life right now? What is it? Are you willing to give the problem to God and trust him to take care of it? Would you tell him that right now?

---

7. Sometimes God takes care of problems in different ways than we would prefer or have imagined. Are you willing to trust him anyway and accept his best outcome whatever it may be?

List three things God has shown you in this chapter that you don't want to forget.

1.

2.

3.

Be the Wave

Lord, from this moment on I commit to . . .

Spend a few minutes talking to God about how you feel. List some specific prayer points that will help you live out the truths in this chapter.

Chapter five

avoiding spiritual slippage

Solomon

It was bizarre enough to make it onto national TV. A bystander had been filming a little league football game. The kids were so small they just looked like helmets with legs. Finally, one of the little helmets emerged from the pack that had been swarming like bees as they chased the ball. He was all alone, carrying a ball almost the same size as he was, running down the field for a certain touchdown. Suddenly a grown man, a parent from the opposing team, ran out onto the field and ruthlessly tackled the young running back, body-slamming him to the ground. I couldn't believe my eyes. That guy needed a reality check. It turned out he was one of those parents who pushed his kid relentlessly to be the best—trying to live through him. It's amazing how many kids have the fun of playing sports sucked from them by parents driving them so hard to succeed.

The expectations could come through sports, grades, looks, college or following the family traditions. In some area of our lives, most of us can probably relate to the pressures to succeed put upon us by our parents. Some of us have parents that are so successful, admired or just plain dominant that it feels like a heavy weight on our lives. How can we measure up? They have worked hard or overcome great odds to succeed and now the pressure is on us to follow in their footsteps and prove ourselves to be even more successful. Perhaps your parents are incredible leaders in their workplace, community or church—you may even be a pastor's kid. How can you measure up to their spiritual accomplishments? Your parents could be plain, hardworking people who dream of a better life for you and have

heaped expectation upon expectation to the point that you feel like you are suffocating under it all.

My father was always in the top of his class at school and went on to be the first in our family ever to attend university. He had a very successful career earning a salary that his parents had only dreamed about. Growing up I felt the shadow of my father's success looming over me. How could I ever live up to his dreams or match his achievements? I sentenced myself to failure before I started. I remember the pressure to go to university, get a degree and "make something of myself" (which usually means gaining fame or money). Sometimes the stress was just too much. I felt like I never measured up.

Many years ago there was a young boy in ancient Israel who knew the same pressures all too well. His father was an incredible success. This father was so loved and adored by everyone that they made him their king. He was one of the most successful military generals of all time; his warriors sang songs of his courage and leadership. Each of them gladly would have died for him. His spiritual devotion earned him the title "a man after God's heart." He was such a charismatic leader that people flocked to his side. He could hide in a cave and attract a crowd of people wanting to follow him. As a business leader he spearheaded an economic transformation of a small confederation of farmers into an established nation of commerce. Loved by king and country as a poor shepherd boy, he was now idolized as a rich and powerful world leader. That's a tough act to follow.

Solomon knew the pressures of growing up in King David's palace from an early age. He always felt he had to prove his right to be there. He felt like an outsider who didn't really fit. Everyone knew about the scandalous events preceding his birth. His brothers and sisters constantly reminded him of it. Most of them were much older and didn't want anything to do with him. They just saw him as competition for their

father's attentions. Though King David was a great leader, he struggled to show the love and attention his kids longed for. He was an absent father, withdrawn and distant. His soldiers saw more of him than his kids did. Everyone struggled for his attention, but they all knew Absalom had been his favorite. The palace would never be the same after Absalom's rebellion. David focused more and more on his work and less and less on his kids. Things were getting out of control.

Solomon often sat on the palace walls and gazed at the people outside in the marketplace as they busily went on with their lives. To them he was a spoiled brat, born with a silver spoon in his mouth. What could he ever do to prove himself? Would they ever accept him for who he was? As a young boy Solomon soon started to feel the pressure of comparison. To the world he would never measure up to King David. His visionary father had accomplished so much, but the dreams of parents for their kids are so much greater. How could he ever live up to his father's expectations and win his approval?

Nobody really understood what it was like to grow up in the palace. Every other kid in the nation dreamed of being in Solomon's place. He, on the other hand, dreamed of being any other boy in the nation. He looked at other kids his age and imagined what it must be like not to have all the tensions. Everyone at home was trying to outperform and outdo the next. Even his mother got caught up in it. Sol felt crushed by it all . . . he felt lonely. Like Solomon many of us live in the self-condemnation of not feeling we could ever measure up, or we are pressured into a path we don't desire. Either way it's a losing proposition. We try our best and are constantly compared to a parent. Many people just self-destruct.

But Sol was not alone. He had a Father in Heaven who loved him, not for what he could do or who he could become. God loved him simply because he existed. Regardless of his parents' background, at the moment Solomon was conceived God had become intimately involved. The heavenly

Father searched the earth for a Solomon and could not find anyone quite like him. So in his wondrous creativity, he called forth exactly what he wanted. Solomon existed because God wanted one of him. Solomon was perfect just the way he was. The heavenly Father saw his isolation and drew near to him. He gave him a special name, Jedidiah (2 Samuel 12:24, 25). *Jedidiah* means "loved by the Lord." God loved Solomon for who he was, not for what he could do. He was the apple of God's eye (see Deuteronomy 32:10; Zechariah 2:8).

What Sol never expected in his wildest dreams happened. The whole nation looked on as young King Solomon stepped forward to offer a sacrifice to God at Gibeon (1 Kings 3). In the midst of a royal struggle and all-out feud, David had finally named his successor. Young Solomon, perhaps only nineteen years old, had just been crowned. He returned to a place of Israel's spiritual heritage, where the tabernacle had been pitched for so many years, to seek God's favor and lead the nation in devotion to the Lord. The whole country assembled to celebrate the great festival. Sol gulped as he looked at this vast multitude of people. He looked deeply into their faces. He saw doubt and concern. How could he, a young man, lead this nation? His grip over the kingdom was still shaky. His own family had not yet fully accepted his appointment, other tribes looked at his position with jealousy and many neighboring nations were surely thinking this inexperienced boy would not possess the military might of his father. He knew his own shortcomings. What if others knew them as well? He was so young, "only a little child" (1 Kings 3:7). Thoughts like these filled his mind as he tossed and turned, trying to sleep . . . until God showed up, in a dream.

Ask for whatever you want me to give you. **1 Kings 3:5**

If that had been me, I think I would have grabbed my list of needs and desires and started reeling them off. I wish I could say I would have replied as well as Sol did. His thoughts were not on himself but were rooted in a passion to live for God. He wanted to fulfill God's dream, to seize his destiny and see his generation become greater than the last—to see his and the next generation impact the kingdom of God. He realized if he was going to be the best leader he could be, he needed help—and plenty of it!

Solomon asked for wisdom. What is wisdom? Is it the accumulation of knowledge over many years? Is it the ability to spout off a pithy saying that has little relevance to the issue at hand? Is it based on how many degrees I have and what subjects they are in? The Bible says that it is none of these. Wisdom comes directly from God (Proverbs 2:6). It is more than just gathering data and knowledge—it is how that knowledge is used. Wisdom is the ability to judge a situation correctly and to apply knowledge and understanding in the light of God's will. It's not just knowing what God says; it's rightly applying what God says to the right situation, at the right time.

If any of you lacks wisdom, he should ask God, who gives generously to all without finding fault, and it will be given to him. **James 1:5**

Solomon committed his life to God and was giving it everything he had. News of his passion, commitment and dedicated life spread far and wide. The nation prospered as God blessed Sol's rule. If we will trust God and be a generation characterized by wisdom (rightly applying God's Word to our situations), we will walk in his blessing. Our lives will reflect it, our generation will reflect it, our world will be affected—and we will embrace our destiny as a generation greater than the last.

Solomon began well, but along the way he tripped up. The important thing is not just how we start a race but also how we finish it. At the

beginning of a race all the runners are jockeying for position, ready to explode off the line. The adrenaline is pumping as they mentally focus on the race and its course. When the gun fires, they burst forward in a mass of energy. At first they crowd one another as they pound along, lap after lap, mile after mile. Then muscles begin to tire and concentration lapses—suddenly fatigue sets in and they slip. They started with such energy, determination and confidence. What went wrong? They started well but did not prepare themselves to finish well.

Solomon rose to the challenge to dedicate his life to God—to be a history maker. He started full of passion, but then just as things looked like they were going so well . . . he slipped. It was just a little at first. But that's where it all begins. We begin to slip when we allow our focus to stray ever so slightly and think, *I'm just going to go to this party, or date that person. I'm just going to go a little further than I should in case he thinks I'm a loser and dumps me. I'm just going to check out that Web site, that chat room, or that movie . . . I know I shouldn't, but it will be OK, just this once. It will be fine, I can handle it, everyone else does it.*

For Solomon the slippage began by marrying Pharaoh's daughter (I Kings 3:1). Solomon knew that God did not want him to marry a foreign wife. It was *unwise* because she would bring foreign gods into their home, into their nation . . . and pull his heart away from the Lord. But he did it anyway. He lost his footing, just a little. I think Solomon was a victim of the counterfeit of God's wisdom . . . worldly wisdom. If God's wisdom is defined as rightly applying his Word to our situations, then the counterfeit is doing what seems right in the eyes of people. According to the wisdom of the world, Solomon's move seemed like good strategy. It was a good political move to make an alliance with the powerful nation of Egypt. It ensured security and opened the way for trade and great financial gain. Solomon led Israel into a golden age, and much of the trade came through Egypt. To outsiders it looked like he was on pace to set a world record.

It's easy to rush into a future propelled by counterfeit wisdom. We

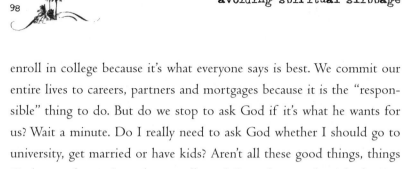

enroll in college because it's what everyone says is best. We commit our entire lives to careers, partners and mortgages because it is the "responsible" thing to do. But do we stop to ask God if it's what he wants for us? Wait a minute. Do I really need to ask God whether I should go to university, get married or have kids? Aren't all these good things, things God wants for us? Sure, they are all good. Sure, they may be right for you. But have you asked? What if God has a different path for you? Something better, something greater. Worldly wisdom tells us we don't even have to think about this stuff. It's all good responsible stuff—it's what everyone does. Then by the time we realize that God may have had a better plan for our lives, it's too late. Many people miss their God-given destinies because they simply didn't stop to ask. By the time they realize that there may have been more . . . they have a mortgage, bills, a family. The dream dies. God's wisdom for your life may be a different route, one you will never regret. Stop and ask God what *he* wants.

So where can you find someone truly wise, truly educated, truly intelligent in this day and age? Hasn't God exposed it all as pretentious nonsense?
1 Corinthians 1:20, The Message

The world missed God when he showed up in human form because they were looking with worldly wisdom. They were looking for what they thought God should look like. Can you imagine Jesus being around today? Most of the time he was homeless and worked odd jobs as a casual laborer here and there. Instead of carrying on the family carpentry business, he left his family to spend time with his newfound friends. He constantly caused trouble at church, was given to acts of vandalism and told people that he believed himself to be God! He didn't care about working to put a roof over his head or food on the table, and he missed a few engagements because he

allowed himself to be interrupted. If anyone needed a PDA it was Jesus. Can you imagine what the world would say to him? Get a job, a place to live, provide for your family, cut your hair, don't you care what people think? Finally, he died as a common criminal. How irresponsible was that?

Are universities, marriage, kids and mortgages bad? No. The issue is motive. What motivates our decisions—worldly wisdom or God? Are we rightly applying God's desires in our situation, or are we conforming to the pressures of the world? Hebrews 11 is full of people who, by the world's wisdom, got it all wrong. But in God's eyes they are heroes of faith. The issue is *trust*. Do we trust that God loves us more than we love ourselves? Do we believe he can do a better job of providing for us, taking care of our needs and our futures? For Solomon it all began when he doubted this very thing and began to act for himself. "I will just do this one thing . . . it will be fine." Solomon lost his footing even though he had been warned,

But if you or your descendants abandon me and disobey my commands and laws, and if you go and worship other gods, then I will uproot the people of Israel from this land I have given them. **1 Kings 9:6, 7,** NLT

God told Solomon that if he were ever to turn from him and stop acting wisely, then God would cut off Israel from the land he had given them. One foreign wife led to 700 wives and 300 concubines—unmarried sexual partners! And, sure enough, it happened . . .

As Solomon grew old, his wives turned his heart after other gods, and his heart was not fully devoted to the LORD his God. . . . He followed Ashtoreth the goddess of the Sidonians, and Molech the detestable god of the Ammonites. So Solomon did evil in the eyes of the LORD. **1 Kings 11:4-6**

How did the wisest man in the world slip? Slowly. It was a gradual slide. Do you know how to boil a frog? Do it gradually. If you throw a frog into a pan of boiling water, it will leap right back out. But if you put the frog in a pan of cool water and gradually turn up the heat, he will boil alive. How can we be careful not to slip? Stay focused. If we allow our attention to wander, our affection soon follows, which will alter our direction.

Attention

But as for me, my feet had almost slipped; I had nearly lost my foothold. For I envied the arrogant when I saw the prosperity of the wicked.
Psalm 73:2, 3

Watch your footing. We need to keep our attention on God, not on others around us. You know the old saying "The grass is always greener on the other side." If we look at the lives and actions of others and begin to think, *I wish I could do that* or *Perhaps I should do that too*, we begin to slip. Solomon took his attention off God and began to focus on the prosperous nations around him. He wanted to be like them, so he started to act like them. If we are envying other people, we're not trusting God's plan for our lives. We have to keep our focus and our trust on God.

Without wavering, let us hold tightly to the hope we say we have, for God can be trusted to keep his promise. **Hebrews 10:23, NLT**

The runners were rounding the corner, neck and neck. It would be an all-out sprint to the finish line. Digging deep, they forced every ounce of energy and speed. Suddenly, one of the runners was distracted by something in the grandstand. He momentarily glanced up to see what it

was. As he looked up he began to stray toward the grandstand, out of his lane and into the path of the other runners. In the blink of an eye several runners collided, sprawling helplessly on the red dirt. We tend to veer toward our focus. Our swerve begins as we focus on something else and lose our concentration.

Affection

Our hearts will soon follow our eyes. Solomon had so much to prove to the world. He desperately wanted to step out from his father's long shadow. His attention slipped as he glanced at the nations around him, and his heart soon followed. He stopped trusting God and began to trust in the world. As his attention was diverted toward the surrounding nations, his heart followed and he began to worship their gods. If we take our eyes off God and look at the world around us, it won't be long before we are chasing after its idols. Like Solomon, we will be influenced by the world rather than by God. If we stop trusting God with every detail of our lives, we will soon start wandering.

Direction

Solomon completely lost his direction. He started out fully following God, trusting him for every detail. He ended doing "evil in God's sight." More importantly, the entire nation lost its direction as well. Solomon introduced idol worship to the nation. The nation lost its focused attention, its affection followed as it fell in love with idols and stopped trusting God, and its direction ultimately became the destruction of the nation. Our attention will have an impact on a nation, either positively or negatively. Here are some pointers to help keep you running toward the right goal.

A runner is familiar with the course before he starts the race. As he becomes familiar with the course, he establishes some *points of reference*, perhaps a building or natural landmark. These points of reference help keep the

runner on the right track and heading in the right direction. They can also be used to gauge progress, time and position. As the runners become familiar with the course, they also notice areas to avoid. Finally, the reference points help the runners find their bearings so they can refocus, should their attention slip momentarily. We also need to be familiar with the course we are running. Our course map is the Bible. We must be familiar with it, find points of reference in it to be sure we are running in the right direction.

A good runner has a *coach* to guide and encourage. In the midst of a race, it is easy to lose perspective and start running too fast or too slowly. A coach stands back and sees the big picture. The mentor can maintain perspective on the race and inform, guide, counsel and encourage the runner in moments of uncertainty and fatigue. In the middle of the Christian race, it's easy to lose perspective. Our position is constantly changing, and our points of reference are often hidden. We too need a coach, a trusted friend who can tell us where we are heading and any areas we should avoid. The outside input can help direct us back onto our chosen course or encourage us when we are struggling. This guidance may come from a pastor, a parent or a friend—someone we trust to hold us accountable and encourage us in the race. If you are going to run to win, you can't do it without help.

Ultimately, the runner must maintain focus by *looking ahead*. A good runner is thinking about what's ahead, not just about where he is or has been. He will not be distracted or detoured. If we are to reach the finish line, we too must fix our eyes on the finish line ahead of us and run without distractions. One of the worst things we can do is look back. If we look back too often or for too long, we will slip. Keep your focus and run without swerving.

You may feel hopeless because you've already slipped. Perhaps it's only a little, or perhaps you stopped running some time ago. Your race is not over. God is still cheering you on. You are not disqualified or out of the running.

When I said, "My foot is slipping," your love, O LORD, supported me.

Psalm 94:18

If you have slipped, jump up and get back in the race. I often slip and fall—I have spiritual scabs all over my knees where I have often tripped up. I get tired; sometimes I look over my shoulder and stumble. We will fall into temptation and sin. When we do, we must realize it does not stop God from believing in us and cheering for us. Julian of Norwich observed, "God does not want us to despair because we fall often and grievously; for our falling does not hinder him in loving us."

God is not upset at our falling. He is heartbroken when we fall and then feel like we cannot run to him for comfort and healing. God blessed Solomon, knowing that he would slip. Jesus chose the disciples, knowing they all would abandon him in his hour of need. God expects you to fall more than you expect it yourself. But he also knows that you can jump up and get back in the race.

If you've fallen and your knees are muddy, it's OK. The night before Jesus died, he was in the upper room with the disciples and began to wash their feet. Peter felt embarrassed and did not want Jesus touching his pinkies. Jesus warned Peter to allow this symbolic act. So Pete asked for a full bath! Here is Jesus' response:

A person who has had a bath needs only to wash his feet; his whole body is clean. And you are clean. **John 13:10**

In those days houses didn't have showers and baths in them. Everyone went to the public baths. Walking home after a nice, long soak, your feet (wearing only sandals) got dirty from the dry, dusty roads. By the time you got home, both your feet would be filthy with the dust. So on arrival people

would rewash their feet, rinsing off the dust. They didn't need another bath; they were still clean—they just had dusty feet. If you are a Christian, you've already had a bath—you are squeaky clean and smelling good. But as you walk in this fallen world, you are going to slip from time to time and get your feet dirty. You are still clean, just like Peter; you just need Jesus to wash your feet. When we ask Jesus to forgive us, he rinses our feet off (1 John 1:9). He doesn't have to give us a complete bath again. You see, you are not dirty through and through. You just have dirt on you. Wash it off, and get back in the race.

Think of a sparkling brand-new mirror. If you were to stand in front of it, you would see a crystal clear image of yourself. But leave that mirror outside for a month or two, and it would be really hard to see yourself. Your image would be distorted and clouded by the dirt and dust. But the mirror is *not* filthy. It just has dirt on it. You can wash the mirror and the dirt comes right off. Your brilliant reflection is restored. The mirror itself was not dirty. The dirt had not become part of the mirror. It was just on the mirror, affecting the reflection. When you slip and get your feet dirty, you are not *dirty*. You just have dirt on you, and that can be rinsed off. The dirt does not become part of you; it does not define you.

We'd better get on with it. Strip down, start running—and never quit! No extra spiritual fat, no parasitic sins. Keep your eyes on Jesus, who both began and finished this race we're in. Study how he did it. Because he never lost sight of where he was headed—that exhilarating finish in and with God—he could put up with anything along the way.

Hebrews 12:1, 2, THE MESSAGE

God is right beside us, willing us to finish. Shake off any condemnation or feelings of insecurity. *Refocus.* Get up and start running again—don't

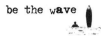

worry about where you were or where you could be or should be. Just set your eyes on the finish line and refocus. Run like the wild, crazy, forgiven, loved, child of God that you are.

And smile.

Making Waves

---

1. Have you ever felt so pressured to succeed at something that you began to dread the very thing you loved? How did it make you feel? How can you regain the desire without the pressure?

---

2. Are your parents' expectations for your future stressing you out? Have you told them how pressured you feel?

---

3. What are some specific areas in your life in which you know what God desires but you are not doing it? How can you change that?

---

4. What are you focusing on right now?

---

5. List three people (people you respect, trust, and who love God) you can ask to keep you accountable and help you avoid slipping.

---

6. Have there been times when you acted unwisely and did something you know you shouldn't have done? Did it work out for good or bad? Have you asked God to forgive you?

---

7. List some practical things you can do to help refocus on Jesus.

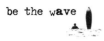

List three things God has shown you in this chapter that you don't want to forget.

1.
_____

_____

2.
_____

_____

3.
_____

_____

Be the Wave

Lord, from this moment on I commit to . . .

Spend a few minutes talking to God about how you feel. List some specific prayer points that will help you live out the truths in this chapter.

_____

_____

_____

_____

_____

_____

_____

_____

_____

Chapter six

knowing the will of God

Esther

It was a hot, sticky afternoon in the dusty little village in northern India. A small team of young Christians had just arrived to spend two weeks performing community service and sharing their faith. Soon after their arrival, a village leader confronted them.

"I forbid you to speak about Jesus in our village!"

Shocked, the team went back to their sweltering little room, gathered under the slow, squeaking ceiling fan—and prayed. What should they do? They felt that God had called them to share with these people; they must obey a higher law. Being sensitive to the cultural differences, they humbly served the community and waited for the right opportunities to share their faith. A few days later the village elder returned. This time he brought the police with him. They arrested the team on the spot and took them to a jail cell in an old tower-like building. Before locking the cell door, the man coldly said to the frightened prisoners, "I told you not to speak of this Jesus. You will spend the night in this cell and tomorrow one of you will die. You have the night to decide who it will be."

As the man turned to leave, a member of the group timidly spoke up. With trembling voice he asked, "What would it take for you to believe in our God?"

Without a moment's pause the elder turned on his heel. "Rain," he answered. "We have not had rain in months. Our crops are failing and people are starving."

In that moment a balloon of faith welled up in the young team member.

His scratchy voice betrayed his nervousness, "Tomorrow before you return you will see rain, and it will be the tears of passion of our God for you."

"As you say," replied the elder. "But if not, *two* of you shall die and you will choose who." Then he slammed and bolted the heavy cell door.

The team was paralyzed with fear. In stunned silence they began to cry out to God in desperation. They prayed throughout the night. Hour after hour slipped away, and still they begged and pleaded with God. It was late into the night when one of the team felt God was giving them a word of encouragement from Mark 10:51. They turned to the passage and read the words of Jesus,

What do you want me to do for you? Mark 10:51

They were filled with a sense of anticipation as they cried out for rain. Faith slowly grew with dawn fast approaching. Praises and worship rose in their hearts until all glorified God in one voice. Whether it rained or not, they still would worship God . . . because he was worth it. Even if it meant giving their lives, they would trust the Father's will. Silence filled the cell as they waited, wondering when the man would return.

Out of nowhere there was a *plop* on the roof, then another, followed by another. Dark clouds engulfed the clear skies. It was a torrential downpour.

"Friends!"

The voice seemed distant, drowned out by the rain, but there it was again. "Friends!"

Looking through the small, barred window, they could see the village elder down below. It had rained so much that he had to come by boat.

"Friends," he shouted out with tears streaming down his face. "I have come on the tears of passion of your God to worship him!"

Following God's will for our lives can seem so thrilling when we look

back at having done it, but at the time it can be confusing and challenging. Many years before the birth of Jesus, a young girl experienced the thrill and challenge of finding the answers. Her name was Esther.

Esther ached with loneliness. Her parents had both died when she was very young. She sat by herself on a shaded wall, watching other kids walk past, hand in hand with their moms and dads. They looked so happy. The sweet smell of jasmine brushed her cheeks as a warm breeze slipped past. Esther took a deep breath and then sighed. Why did God take both of her parents and leave her alone? She longed to have a normal family like the other kids, but she was forced to brave the world alone. The life of a street orphan was full of challenges and perils. It was a constant daily battle for survival. Cheat disease and you were forced to battle hunger. Overcome loneliness and you were confronted with violence. Not many kids lasted long on the cruel streets. The only hope was to join a gang of other unwanted street kids to find shelter and protection in a makeshift family.

The challenge was even greater for a girl. Girls were weak and vulnerable. Esther would not find acceptance or compassion from any of the young orphan boys. Where could she go, what could she do to escape? If someone did not step in on her behalf, she would be doomed. Providentially, someone did. Esther didn't have to face the prospect of life on the streets. Her elder cousin Mordecai took her in. She wouldn't have to spend cold nights huddled for shelter in a dark alley or scrounge through garbage for food. She was fortunate and she knew it, but she still longed for her own family. She missed her parents and yearned for her mother's embrace.

Esther held her small bag close to her chest, hugging it like a trusted teddy bear. She felt awkward as she followed her cousin up the stone stairs. She hardly knew him, and now he was all the family she had in the world.

"Well, here we are," he said, pushing open the simple wooden door.

Esther held her breath as she stepped into her new world. The house was

small—just two rooms separated by a short, beaded curtain. There was no furniture, just a couple of mats on either side of the room. A large pot filled with water sat in the corner. A piece of string hung from one wall to the next, laden with clothes drying in the musty heat. During the day this room was the living room, dining room, kitchen and laundry. At night Mordecai hung a white sheet on the string, dividing the room into bedrooms.

"This will be your side; you can keep your things in this wooden chest next to the mat. Just be sure to roll up your things each morning," he said, pointing to the small wooden box.

"Through that door are the toilet and a water jar for showering. If you prefer a bath, I'm afraid you will have to go to the river."

Mordecai smiled awkwardly. He had no idea if young girls preferred to shower or bathe, and now as he looked around, he realized how sterile his home must look to her.

"Er, we can pick up a few things to make the place look a little more like home. If you want, you can come to the market tomorrow and help me choose." He smiled a vaguely confident smile. Esther relaxed and began to unload her bag into the chest. She liked her cousin, even if he was a bit odd.

Days turned into months and months into years.

"You get taller every day!" Mordecai joked. "Are those sandals already too small?"

Esther laughed, "There must be something in the water!"

She had grown to love her cousin. He was funny, loving and respected by everyone in the community. As the sun began to set, Esther and Mordecai climbed the narrow stairs up to the roof where it would be cooler. They sat in the shade eating and looking over the ancient city of Susa, the capital of Persia. Many years before, her grandparents had been taken captive by the Babylonians and forced to leave their home in Israel for a life of slavery in Babylon. The Babylonian Empire eventually fell to the mighty Persians. The Persians were not hard tyrants like their predecessors. The

Jewish people were offered freedom and allowed to return home. But where was home? The older generation had all but died out. For the rest, this was home. Israel was a distant and precarious place and few returned. So like most of the Jewish people, Mordecai and Esther remained in Persia where Mordecai had a good job serving the king as a gatekeeper.

In many ways Esther was a lot like you and me. She dreamed of what the future would hold. Would she fall in love and have a family of her own? What would her husband be like? Would she be famous? What was God's will for her life? What was her destiny? How would she navigate the road of God's will for her life?

It was all over the news. Everyone was talking about it. The king of Persia was on the lookout for a new wife. Every corner shop was buzzing with the latest gossip. The king had decided to hold his very own beauty pageant. Young girls from all over Persia were being brought to the palace to compete.

"Esther, you've got mail," her cousin said, a little surprised as he rummaged through the stack at breakfast.

Esther opened the letter and her heart froze. The hairs on the back of her neck stood stiff. Her mind started to swim. The last thing she remembered was a feeling of nausea overwhelming her and then everything went blank. She hit the ground like a sack of potatoes. Her head throbbed as she slowly opened her eyes. Mordecai was leaning over her with a damp cloth pressed to her forehead. Esther was overwhelmed with a feeling she had not known since she was a little girl sitting on a wall watching families. The letter was a summons to the palace. But how? Who had even noticed a shy, awkward orphan girl?

As she walked through the palace gates, Esther felt confused and very nervous. What would happen to her? What did all this mean? When would she see her cousin again? Would she ever be allowed to return to her safe little home? What if the king wasn't pleased with her? Then again, what if

he *was?* She was led into a large, marble room. It was a comfortable room with lots of soft pillows and a fountain gently trickling in the middle. Tables were laden with sumptuous fruit and the finest vegetables. Esther's focus was on all the other young girls there with her. *There must be dozens of us here,* she thought aloud. Finally a gong sounded and a short, fat man, who was well-dressed and seemed very self-important, waddled into the room. He cleared his throat loudly, then spoke, "For the next twelve months, this will be your new home. You must not leave. During this time you will be prepared to go before the king. Then he will decide."

Twelve months? I have to stay here a year? That's a lifetime! Esther felt sick to her stomach as waves of depression came over her. She longed to go home, back to the security of her cousin and her safe little life. For the next twelve months she would have to undergo beauty treatments, practice walking like a queen, and, of course, work on her talent! Should she sing or maybe dance? (Could you imagine taking a year to get ready to go out for an evening on the town?) When her turn came she would be taken to the king's private rooms. If he really liked her, he would take her for his wife. She looked at the beautiful marble rooms, the richly appointed beds and the bathtubs! It was just like a fairy tale—a common girl who became a princess.

Sound romantic? I doubt it. Esther had no choice in all this. Unlike other fairy tales, Esther had not fallen in love with her Prince Charming. She hadn't even met him! He wasn't all that charming either. The king was not interested in winning her heart. He didn't pace the floor thinking of romantic schemes to overwhelm her with love and affection. He either enjoyed her physically, or she would spend the rest of her life locked in his harem, knitting socks and hoping the phone might ring. Esther had been ripped away from her life, family and friends—thrown into a new and strange world where she no longer had any control over her decisions. All she had left was her trust in God. He *was* in control of her life, right? She had always believed

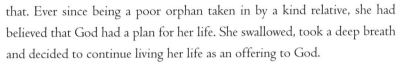

that. Ever since being a poor orphan taken in by a kind relative, she had believed that God had a plan for her life. She swallowed, took a deep breath and decided to continue living her life as an offering to God.

Every day for twelve long months Esther gazed into the sky and thought of home. The walls were so high. All she had seen for months was the bright blue sky. She felt desperately lonely. Why was she even there? She looked around at the other girls primping and preparing. They all seemed prettier and more talented. Esther felt so empty. She even had to keep her faith hidden. The other girls just talked about all the shopping they could do with a royal charge card. It was tough, but she would trust and follow her heavenly Father. She continued to mark days, weeks and months off the calendar.

Finally, the big day arrived. It was her turn to go before the king. She was given her choice of whatever clothing or jewelry she wanted. She was so nervous she could hardly eat a thing. The royal dining room was so big, and the king was at the far end.

After spending the night with the king, Esther was brought back to the harem, where the king's wives lived. She would stay there the rest of her days—unless the king had really enjoyed her and requested for her again.

That morning the short, fat guy who was in charge of the beauty pageant announced, "The rest of the pageant is cancelled, the king has chosen . . . Esther!"

The months of hard work had paid off. The king was physically attracted to Esther—she was beautiful—but there was something else about this girl. She had a presence, a depth, and she soon won royal favor and approval. God had raised Esther up from orphan to mother of a nation.

Every young girl dreams of being a princess, and Esther was no different. When she was a little girl, her cousin would take her to see the beautiful palace and fountains. She would clutch his hand, close her eyes and dream of being a princess—to have beautiful clothes and sleep on a bed of soft,

luxurious cushions. Surely that was just a childish fantasy . . . she rubbed her eyes and pinched herself expecting to wake up any minute. It was real; she was a queen—of a mighty empire.

The wedding was like a bedtime story. Vibrant flowers overflowed in every room of the palace. The halls were rich with an aroma of the finest spices and draped in shimmering silks and flowing linen. Every citizen of Susa and people from all over the empire lined the streets to take in the event. The entire nation ground to a halt to tune in to the spectacle. Esther was the people's queen. A young commoner, one of them, was about to be crowned. People jostled in the streets as they lined up to wave their flags, hoping to catch a glimpse of her carriage as it passed. The deafening cheers and trumpet blasts moved along the crowd in pace with the carriage. Her long gown flowed behind her as her attendants entered and glided down the aisle. It was like a dream, and every citizen of the empire was invited.

Esther didn't have long to adjust to her new life before its purpose became clear. Her position as queen was not simply by chance. God had a destiny for her to fulfill. Haman, a wicked adviser and close confidant to the king, felt threatened by Mordecai. Haman vowed to take his revenge by annihilating the entire Jewish population. Like a snake he deceptively slithered through the shadows of the palace laying his plan. Then, when the time was perfect, he deceived the king to write it as law. Nothing could stop the massacre now—nothing except the move of God. Esther didn't know it yet, but she was the only hope for her people.

Esther trembled with fear as she heard the news. She had just become queen only to discover her entire nation was to be killed . . . including her! What could she do? She was not trained for this. She was too young and unprepared. Surely somebody else handled stuff like this. Where are the adults when you need them? How would this affect her new position? Her mind reeled. She had to talk to her cousin. Mordecai burst into the queen's chambers. He threw his arms around her and cried, "My little Esther

. . . a beautiful queen. Oh, if only your mother could have seen this." They caught up on all the latest happenings in the old neighborhood as they sipped their tea.

"You've heard the news?" Mordecai asked tentatively. Then without drawing breath he challenged her,

---

Maybe you were made queen for just such a time as this.

Esther 4:14, THE MESSAGE

Esther spat out her tea. "What? You've got to be joking!"

Esther wanted to follow God's will, but how could she know what it was? She needed insight, and fast! She prayed, fasted, sought input from others to check her motives, looked for confirmation and finally moved forward, listening for directions. She could be confident she was firmly in the will of God—she could not make a mistake. Esther felt it was God's will to approach the king and plead for her people. It would be dangerous; if the king were displeased, it would cost her life. She would not hide in her newfound luxury but risk it all to be in God's will.

I will go to the king. . . . And if I perish, I perish. **Esther 4:16**

Esther was prepared to lay her life on the line. Even if it cost her life, she knew that God was in control. Knees trembling and palms sweating, she approached the throne room. It had been months since she had even seen the king. Perhaps she had done something wrong and upset him. She tried to stop her mind from racing ahead. Would the king be in a good mood? She prayed no one had brought him bad news that day. Her stomach knotted up and her heart thumped in her chest as the doorman announced

her arrival. Would he be pleased by her uninvited visit? Would she live or die?

Navigating the Highway of God's Will

Prepare for the Trip

Simon son of John, do you truly love me? **John 21:15**

Before taking off on a road trip, it's always wise to give the car a thorough check—things like the oil and water levels and tire pressure. Before beginning the journey into God's will, we need to do a heart check. Whether Peter truly loved Jesus was more important than what he could do for Jesus. Are we living for God in response to his love for us? God's primary desire for us is that we know him. God is more interested in us as his children than in what we can do for him. The most important thing about a road trip is who you're with. Do you know what God really wants? He wants to know you—to hang out with you. He doesn't care where you've been, what you've done, what you wear or how many piercings you have! He is not that interested in what we can do for him—he *is* God after all; he can manage. God's first desire is friendship, a living and intimate relationship where we are free to share every fear, concern and joy. First Thessalonians 4:3 tells us that God's will is that we be sanctified. *Sanctified* means to be "set apart." It is like being in an exclusive relationship. Tiger Woods has an exclusive contract with Nike® for his clothing—he is sanctified to Nike®. We are set apart for God; we are in an exclusive love relationship with him.

Check the Route

Delight yourself in the LORD and he will give you the desires of your heart.
Psalm 37:4

How do we know what to do, specifically? Well, what do you want to do? I believe that God places desires in our hearts. What would you really love to do? Whatever it is, it's probably directly from the Father's heart, just for you—so do it for his glory. Trust that he has put those passions in your heart. Think about it this way: if you took a bunch of people and asked them to do something they really didn't want to do, how do you think it would turn out? Nobody would be happy, productivity would be low and everyone would be complaining. But what if you took the same group and let them do what they really wanted to do? They would do it with all their hearts. People would try their best, everyone would be fulfilled and no one would be grumbling. God is the author of "smart"—he gives us our desires, then releases us to them. Productivity goes up and it's a lot less grief for him. You probably have a crazy dream buried deep inside you somewhere. Believe that it is from God, trust him and go for it!

Get Going

The next step is to try a few different things. Take a few test drives. Kick a few tires. Hang out with a pastor for a month and see if that is what you want to do with your life. Go on a short-term mission trip. Intern at a business and see what is right for you. Here's a good rule of thumb: if you enjoy doing it and other people enjoy your doing it, you're onto something. You get only one shot at this thing called life. It is worth taking the time and expense to find what you really want to do. Be an original.

Listen for Directions

What happens when we come to a crossroads? Which way should we go? We need to listen for directions. God's will is not a formula when it comes to the specific choices in our lives, such as where we live, what we do, whom we marry and when. For the last few weeks, I have been trying to figure out how to make cold coffee drinks at home that taste just like Starbucks® and other coffee shops. But there's some secret ingredient I am missing. It just doesn't taste quite like the real thing. Sometimes we think God's will is like mixing ingredients. If we forget the smallest thing, it will all be ruined. We think we will have missed God's will forever. That's not true. God's will is dynamic and ever-changing. God even takes into account our mistakes (Romans 8:28). You don't have to settle for second-best in your life because you made a mistake a year ago. God's perfect will is permissive. Otherwise one mistake I make would throw the entire universe off. His will for my life (which is perfect) allows for (permits) my missing a turn or running a red light every now and again. If you're living for God with all your heart—it's never second best.

We tend to think of God's will as a kind of cosmic yellow-brick road. We get worried when a decision comes up. How will I know which way to turn? What if I don't hear God's voice? Will I ever see him again or get back to the right road? Wait a minute. Is there anywhere God isn't? Could I really turn right and find that God is only on the left? That would seriously limit God. Here's the good news—God can stop us from making the wrong choice. If God's presence in our lives is determined entirely by whether we make the right choice in every circumstance, then God is very limited. If you are walking in a relationship with God, he is big enough to let you know if he doesn't want you to be an actor or a plumber. If there is something specific, he will put the desire in your heart. God is not limited to a single path—he lives in you. Wherever you go he is right there. More

important than the road we travel is the company we keep. It's about the trip, the relationship—not the destination. That's why he doesn't just lay out every choice for the next fifty years of our lives. If he did we would jump in our car, throw the top down, wave good-bye and be gone in a cloud of dust. He wants to share the trip with us. The relationship in the midst of making the choices in our lives is the most important thing to our Father. Here is a six-point checklist you can use when you get to those crossroads.

1. Will my choice be in line with God's general will? That's what he's already revealed in the Bible. For instance, I can be assured God is not calling me to be a professional bank robber (Exodus 20:15) or to have sexual encounters before marriage (I Thessalonians 4:3). I'm not the king of a pagan nation. Check.

2. The next step is to pray. God said,

Call to me and I will answer you and tell you great and unsearchable things you do not know. Jeremiah 33:3

Quite often we know what God is saying. The question is, will we do it? Sometimes his will is scary, but we have to trust he knows what is best and that we will not miss his will. Check.

3. What do you *want* to do? As long as our desire is within God's general will, it's probably from him. Look up Psalm 37:4-6. There are two pieces of good news here. First, if we delight in God, he will give us the passions and desires that rise up within us. Secondly, he will give us those desires . . . he will allow us to follow our dreams.

Commit to the L<small>ORD</small> whatever you do, and your plans will succeed.

Proverbs 16:3

There's probably something you would really love to do with your life. You would give anything to be involved in it . . . it's your dream. If you want to do it to glorify God, then what are you waiting for? Check.

4. Check your motive.

Plans fail for lack of counsel, but with many advisers they succeed.

Proverbs 15:22

Also check out Proverbs 11:14; 13:10. Talk to some people you trust. People who love you will be ready to test your motives and tell you truthfully what they think. Find some wise old sages whom you respect and who really know and love God. They will be able to help you process and check your motives. This is a great way to hear from God and get confirmation from several sources. They will also become a great source of support during some hard turns. Check.

5. Look for confirmation. When I turn onto an unfamiliar road, the first thing I look for is a sign to confirm I'm on the right road and going in the right direction. Ask God to confirm the decision. Look for signs in the Bible and through others . . . listening for God's voice. Check.

6. Make the choice. If your choice is built on the checklist above, you can be confident you are in his will. You won't make a mistake, because the whole point is a deeper relationship. By going through this process, you have been intimate with God. You have encountered him en route, and that

is the whole point. Focus on God, not on guidance. There is a lot more freedom regarding God's will than most people realize. In various situations there are many choices that can be made, and you know what? They are all right. Who knows what wild desires and dreams God has for you? Buckle up, hang on and—have a nice trip!

As at first, God gave Esther favor with the king. In fact the king was so pleased to see her that he offered her up to half of his kingdom. Ultimately, Esther saved her people. Haman's evil scheme was exposed, and Mordecai was made president of the empire, second only to the king. Esther found her destiny as she rested in God's destiny. Who could have imagined that this young orphan girl would navigate the highway of God's will to save an entire nation of people from total annihilation?

Making Waves

---

1. Read Romans 12:1, 2. Have you been living like an original or conforming to the pressures to act like the world? List the reasons why. What will you do about it?

---

2. List some things that are God's general will for your life (things God has already told us in the Bible). Rate yourself on each of these from 1 to 10. How can you improve?

---

3. Do you feel God is specifically prompting you to do something? Has he told you what it is?

---

4. How have you sought confirmation?

---

5. What was the last thing God asked you to do? Did you do it?

---

6. Do you feel God's prompting you to do something you have been reluctant to do? Why? What is it and will you do it now?

---

7. Do you have a crazy dream you would love to do? Share it with someone.

List three things God has shown you in this chapter that you don't want to forget.

1.

2.

3.

Be the Wave

Lord, from this moment on I commit to . . .

Spend a few minutes talking to God about how you feel. List some specific prayer points that will help you live out the truths in this chapter.

Chapter seven

hearing the voice of God

Mary

The sense of anticipation and excitement was overwhelming as the small group huddled together, though an eerie silence clung to the room. Would God really speak? What would he say? How would they recognize him if he did? Everyone focused on listening, but what were they listening for? A young guy gingerly looked up and peeked around the room. Some of the people were on their knees, arms lifted high as if waiting for the words to literally fall from the sky like snowflakes on a winter's day. Others were spread out flat on the floor, propping their chins up with their fists as they read the Bible. Some seemed so peaceful, about ready to drift off to sleep. Others had such intensity on their faces; it looked as if they were waiting for the results from an exam. The young man rubbed his chin and, closing his eyes, buried his head in his chest. The group was praying for a closed country—a nation where it was a crime to spread the gospel, stage a Bible drama or mention Jesus. Anyone caught disobeying could be punished, imprisoned or even killed.

The leader of the group brought the time to a close. Everyone slowly opened their eyes and looked around at the others. The silence seemed to hang for an eternity as the group stared blankly at one another. No one offered to speak up. A girl in the corner began to fidget and clear her throat. She made such a production out of it, she looked as if she were about to address a room full of dignitaries, not her friends. There was an uneasy air about the group. It felt like everyone had gravely important news to share, but no one dared speak. Finally, someone broke the awkward uneasiness

and quietly said, "Umm . . . I know this is kinda weird, but I think God is telling me to go to this country . . . right now." The fidgety girl exploded to her feet, "Me too!" Then the floodgates opened as everyone in the group began to share their impressions, thoughts and Scripture verses that had come to mind. The excitement, and the noise level, grew as everyone in the group shared how God had told them to go to this particular nation . . . immediately. People shouted, laughed and cried, as they excitedly pointed their fingers at each other in complete amazement. Everyone was talking at once. Everyone, that is, but the leader. He said nothing. One by one the group turned and waited for him to speak. One girl could feel the knots in her stomach tighten as he started to say, "This is weird. I felt God was saying you all should go . . . right away." The final confirmation came from God as he provided visas and all the finances to go, within a few days.

The group gathered again to pray, but this time they huddled in a small, dingy hotel room. It had been less than a week, and now the group sat halfway around the world in the very nation they had interceded for just a few days ago. Their minds raced as anticipation filled the room. What was God going to do? What on earth would *they* do? They were in a closed country. They couldn't just go out and tell everyone about Jesus. Again they went to God. After a time of quietly waiting on God, the group shared their impressions. The consensus was that they should walk the city streets and pray.

They spent the whole first day just walking and praying. The second day they walked, and they prayed. Nothing happened. Doubt began to rear its ugly head. Had they missed God's will? What were they expecting anyway? It was a closed nation! They were not sure what else to do on the third day, so they walked, and they prayed. A couple of young guys walked down a small side street. The road was uneven and full of holes. Dejected and confused, one of the guys began to kick a stone along the curb.

"Pardon. Pardon me. Do you speak English?"

The young men swung round in surprise. Who could that be? A slender woman explained that she had noticed their Western clothes and hoped they might speak English. The guys commented how they didn't expect to hear anyone in this town speak such good English.

"I train English teachers at the college—why don't you and your friends come and speak to my two classes?" the woman replied.

It was just before Christmas, so the teacher asked if they would be willing to explain the meaning of Christmas, as her students did not understand this Western concept. Their mouths fell open. "You bet!"

The next day the team arrived at the school. The first class consisted of thirty people who were training to be English teachers. The team carefully explained the Christmas story, telling them of Christ who came to earth. They told of the same Jesus who had sent them there to share in that classroom, the same Jesus who loved them and desired a relationship with them personally. At the end of the class time, the team led the students in a prayer for salvation. To their surprise all thirty teachers knelt in the middle of the room and asked Jesus into their hearts! The excitement was thick in the air when they prepared for the second class of thirty people. Again all thirty ended the class jumbled together on their knees, crying out to Jesus. All this in a *closed country*! Because this group took the time to listen for God's voice and then trusted that it was God speaking, sixty people met Jesus in a hard-to-reach nation.

Mary grew up in Nazareth—a sleepy, working-class town nestled in the hills west of Galilee. Nazareth had no real industry. There were no lakes to fish, and the chalky, stony hills surrounding it were useless for farming. It was the sort of town young people left as soon as they could go to college—and then never returned. The citizens of Nazareth were plain and poor. Mary's parents were honest, hardworking, devout believers. Ever since she was a baby, Mary had excitedly listened to stories about God and his

chosen people as her dad tucked her into bed. She would snuggle down, her brown eyes wide with anticipation as her dad thoughtfully recalled the historic events. Sometimes he would pretend to forget the ending, and Mary would swing her pillow at him, "beating him" into submission until he promised to finish the epic. As long as she could remember, she had been raised to put her hope in God.

The Romans had invaded Israel by this time and were ruthless rulers. Taxes were high, times were hard and the local governors were often unfair and harsh. For the most part, people kept their heads down to avoid eye contact, trying to remain unnoticed by the Roman soldiers who roamed the streets daily looking for someone to pick on or exploit. Mary often stood at the corner shop and listened to the old women talk about how glorious life was before the Romans. They spoke of golden ages and times of God's presence. Mary spent hours in the synagogue, listening to stories of the great empire of David and Solomon.

Mary's family wasn't snooty, but they had a rich inheritance. She was a descendant of the mighty King David. Royal blood flowed in her veins. Most afternoons Mary roamed through the hills surrounding Nazareth, dreaming of what it would have been like to grow up in the courts of the palace. If only Israel hadn't strayed from God and gone into captivity, she would have known a very different lifestyle. She would have known luxuries, not labor. She would have had beautiful flowing garments—one for each day of the month, rather than the plain robe she wore day in and day out. She would make her way to her favorite spot overlooking the valley, sit on a rock and close her eyes. The warm sun would gently massage her face with its golden rays. Hours would slip away as she sat dreaming. Sooner or later she would hear the faint sounds of Nazareth below and be jolted out of her reverie. The palace was a million miles away from her. Everyone in her town had lost hope. No one expected life to get any better than it was, so how could she? She would never know fame or fortune. Sure, some

people still talked about the coming Messiah who would deliver Israel from Roman domination, but it was a flight of fancy. Anyway, God would not lower himself with a visit to remote Nazareth. No, if God were to show up, it would be many miles away in Jerusalem.

She could dream, but the best Mary could hope for was a simple life far from excitement or adventure. Like every young girl Mary envisioned escaping her drab life in remote Nazareth. She longed for romance and excitement. She dreamt of exotic adventures and locations. But it was just a dream. Young girls had little standing in society. Men were important. Mary's future revolved around marrying, raising children and serving her husband. A woman's role was always subservient to that of men. She had to keep out of sight when visitors were present, serve the men in the family before eating any of the meal herself, fetch water, make clothes, cook the food, and always, always, walk behind while men rode. (Remember the pictures and nativity plays of Joseph and Mary going to Bethlehem? Mary is riding the donkey, right? That is highly unlikely. Joseph would have been the laughingstock of his contemporaries.)

This doesn't mean that women were unloved, simply that it was a man's world. Young girls like Mary didn't even have a say regarding whom they would marry. In most cases marriage arrangements were made while they were still young children. The girls were usually wed in their early teens; the boys were a little older. Imagine growing up in a society where even your meager life is all planned out for you. Not only was Mary living in the hopelessness of the shadow of Rome, she lived in the suffocating grip of a society that treated her as a second-rate citizen.

In fact, Mary was already betrothed to a young man named Joseph. She didn't know much about him. He lived on the other side of town working in his father's carpentry business. He seemed kind, but a little remote—quiet and unassuming. He seemed happy to be in Nazareth and to work in his dad's business. He certainly didn't dream of adventures like

Mary did. He seemed very practical and down-to-earth. He was a good man with a gentle heart and a love for God. She tried to picture her new life as Joe's wife, but it seemed weird. In so many ways she still felt like daddy's little girl; to be married to a strange man was hard to imagine.

As strange as it seemed, she would have to get used to it. Her family had worked long and hard arranging this union. Joe's family traced their heritage directly to King David himself. Joe was a direct descendant from the line of kings. Mary's parents often talked about it with great pride and reminded her how lucky she was. The engagement had been set for one year. In her culture, engagement was as binding as marriage. The only way out was by divorce.

Mary may have dreamed about her life and future, but the reality was that she had little to hope for. It was all decided. What hope did she have of impacting her world? Mary longed to see God move, to see her generation and nation touched by the hand of God. But what could she do? Could she hear God? Surely God would speak to a priest, a rabbi or at least someone like her father. Mary wanted to hear from God, but what could God possibly have to say to a young, insignificant girl like her?

It was late afternoon as Mary crouched in a shady spot on the roof doing the laundry. She aimlessly rubbed the shirt and swirled it around in the soapy water, but her mind was elsewhere. She was lost in thought as she poured out her heart to God. *Lord, it has been 400 years since the last prophet of Israel spoke. Will anything ever change? What will become of my life? Am I destined to be just a housewife? O Lord, I long for something more . . . but I'm just a young girl.* Suddenly, the heavens seemed to tear apart. Light flashed around her from all directions. The noise was as deafening as the cracking of thunder. Mary was thrown backwards, overwhelmed with fear. It felt like the sky was falling in on her. She spun around and sent her bucket crashing, spilling water all over. She was terrified and clung to the bucket for protection as she curled up in the corner, trembling. The light around her seemed as if

it would cut right through her. She covered her eyes with one hand, then lifted it slightly to steal a glance. As she looked her chest tightened, and her heart raced until she thought it would burst. Her mouth fell open but words dried up. She thought she was dying. There before her, hovering in majestic glory, was the angel Gabriel. The creature was beautiful and frightening. His wings sounded like the ocean as they beat the air. His body glowed like bronze. Mary was unable to even move, pinned by the sheer force of his radiance.

Over the roar of his wings, Mary now heard the roar of his voice. As Gabriel spoke, a mighty wind—like that of a helicopter—whipped around, making her eyes water.

Greetings, you who are highly favored! The Lord is with you. Luke 1:28

Mary was flabbergasted. She couldn't believe it.

That is . . . she couldn't believe what he had just said. What had she done to be highly favored? Mary had grown up as a second-class citizen in an afflicted society that could not even rule itself. She was just a young girl who had no say in her own future, let alone in the grand scheme of life. How could she be highly favored? Why would the Lord reveal himself to a nobody like her? She was filled with a whirlwind of emotion—shame, fear, desperation and hope. Could God really be interested in her? Could it be true? The inner turmoil was so strong it was written all over her face. Gabriel repeated his greeting in an attempt to convince her.

Mary, you have found favor with God. Luke 1:30

Mary's mind was still spinning at the intimacy of the greeting. *God knows my name and thinks highly of me?* She was lost in wonder at the thought as

Gabriel continued speaking. Mary's mouth dropped further, and she leaned closer to the angel to see whether she had heard him correctly.

Wait a minute. She was so amazed at the message that she relaxed and forgot that this was her first angelic visitation. *How can I give birth . . . ?*

She bit her lip as she remembered her Uncle Zechariah. Just a few months before, Gabriel had dropped in and told Zech that his aged barren wife would have a child. Zech had questioned Gabriel and lost his tongue for nine months. Mary gulped, but Gabriel simply answered her question. Zech had asked in disbelief. He just couldn't see how his wife's having a child was possibly going to happen. Mary asked for further understanding in faith. She was not discounting the voice of God—she was seeking clarification.

Regardless of our position, age, what we have or haven't done or even our own perception of ourselves, God is with us. He loves us and values us. He favors us highly, and above all, he wants to speak to us. You may feel like Mary. Small. Insignificant. Nobody. Not sure if God is even interested in talking to the likes of you . . . but he is. Will you listen?

You Can Hear God

You may not think you can hear God, but the truth is you already have. If you believe in Jesus, you've already heard that inner voice that drew you to him in the first place. You've already heard the whisper of a passionate father: "You who are highly favored . . . the Lord is with you. I love you. Come to me, let me hold you, feel the rhythm of my heart for you."

Hearing God's voice doesn't have to be hard. We often over-complicate the process. People want to make it sound difficult, as if only they can break through and touch God for you. That was once true. In Old Testament times, only the priest could enter the presence of God. He represented everyone as he went behind the curtain into God's presence. But that is no longer necessary. When Jesus died on the cross, the curtain was ripped

right down the middle (Matthew 27:51). Now we all have personal access to God (Hebrews 10:19-22) in full assurance of acceptance. If you want to obey God and please him, if you want to hear the desires of his heart, it's not hard (John 15:15).

Call to me and I will answer you and tell you great and unsearchable things you do not know. **Jeremiah 33:3**

Before they call I will answer; while they are still speaking I will hear. **Isaiah 65:24**

---

1. Cultivate an Open Heart

The first step in hearing God's voice is to *let God be God*. Be willing to lay aside your thoughts, desires or others' opinions and just listen. Check out Luke 24:13-27. After Jesus' crucifixion, his disciples were walking along, their minds full of the events that had just taken place in Jerusalem. They had jumped to conclusions and were wrestling with so many things. When Jesus approached them he simply asked them, "What things?" (Luke 24:19). That's a strange question if you think about it. He knew better than anyone what had just gone down, so why ask? So they could pour out their thoughts. He gave them the opportunity to get it all out, to tell him everything that was going on. Until they had done so, they wouldn't be able to listen. When we go to God with troubles or questions, the first thing we need to do is just get it all out. Tell him everything and unburden your mind. Take as much time as you want doing this. Be honest with God. He can handle your honesty—and anyway, he already knows what's on your mind. Pour out your ideas, dreams, wishes, fears, problems, pains, hurts, everything—God is an excellent listener.

Then stop.

Don't get up and walk away after you have told him all your stuff. Listen quietly. Jesus waited a long time for the guys to tell him all about the events of the past days, but then they listened as he put it all into perspective. We need to listen as well. Once we have gotten it all out, it is much easier to hear him.

Secondly, *focus on God alone*. Ask God to protect you from the attack of the enemy. Take authority to silence him (James 4:7; Ephesians 6:10-20). Have you ever been praying and suddenly realized that for the last five minutes you've been thinking about some movie, something you're doing later or a recent conversation? Relax. It happens to everyone. Sometimes when we are trying to listen to God, our minds drift. When it happens take the thought captive (2 Corinthians 10:5) and refocus on Jesus. How? Just say to yourself, "Oh man, my mind is wandering. I'll think about that later. Now, God, where were we?" Ask God to help you concentrate on him and hear his voice alone.

Thirdly, *expect God to answer you*. Give him time to speak, just as the apostles on the Emmaus road did. Believe that he wants to speak to you.

The LORD would speak to Moses face to face, as a man speaks with his friend. **Exodus 33:11**

My sheep listen to my voice; I know them, and they follow me.
John 10:27

Mary was hungry for an encounter with God . . . are *we?* Do we want God more than anything else in our lives? Are we hungry for his presence?

The angel reassured Mary that God loved her, was excited about her and wanted to be intimately involved in her life. She could trust that he would not reject her or tell her to come back when she was older and more

responsible. Mary was "highly favored." What had she done to earn such a position? Well, as far as the Bible tells us . . . nothing. She simply hoped in God. You may not have accomplished any great exploits or feel you have earned a special position with God. You may not feel like an awesome prayer warrior or giant in the faith. That's not what God is looking for. He just wants a willing heart that desires him. God is excited about young people who take a stand for him. He is so thrilled when he finds a young man or woman who will lead this generation to the foot of his throne and who will desire genuine worship over the trappings of the world. Just like Mary, you don't need to have done anything mighty for God to receive his favor; it's his gift to those he loves. Understanding that God loves and accepts us before we lift a finger should fuel everything we do from here.

2. Be Open to God's Speaking

The first time God spoke to Mary was through the angel. Later in the account he spoke through the words of her relative Liz. Communication happens in many different ways. It can be a spoken or unspoken word, a look—even a grunt! If you and I communicate in lots of different ways, depending upon the situation or relationship, we should not be surprised to find that God is just as varied in his communication with us. There are two main ways God speaks. The first is called the *rhema* word (*rhema* is a Greek word that can be translated "what is said," "event" or "happening"). It includes stuff like:

• Dreams—When Joseph discovered Mary was pregnant, he was going to divorce her until God spoke to him in a dream (Matthew 1:20). Another Joseph in the Bible saw his future in two dreams (Genesis 37:5-9).

• Visions—Isaiah's vision changed his life radically (Isaiah 6:1-13). God also spoke to Peter through a vision (Acts 10:9-15).

• Audible voice—God spoke to the people of Israel at Mt. Sinai (Exodus 19), to Samuel when he was young (1 Samuel 3), to Jesus and those

with him at his baptism (Matthew 3:17) and to Paul (Acts 9).

• Angels—We often read about angelic beings bringing the word of God to people (Daniel 9:21; Luke 1:26-28; 2:9-12).

• A word of wisdom or knowledge (1 Corinthians 12:8).

• Still, small voice—Probably the most common method of hearing God is intuition with a spiritual message. Sometimes it is a strong sense, a feeling of direction or a download of information. God spoke to the prophet Elijah in this way (1 Kings 19:11-13).

• Circumstances—Circumstances should not be used for your primary guidance, but as confirmation. Sometimes we must push through our circumstances for the breakthrough. Just because things become difficult it does not mean we need to give up or that it's not God's will.

• Counsel of others—This also should be a confirmation of something God is already saying to us. The Bible says we should share with godly and wise people what we believe God is saying to us. They can examine our ideas and look at them from a different perspective; this protects us and helps us be sure of our motives. Sometimes when we are so close to our situation, it is hard to get clear guidance. The godly counsel of others can help us see clearly (Proverbs 13:10; 15:22).

The second way God speaks to us is through his *written* Word. This is the most important way God communicates. Sometimes we struggle to know God's will when he has already told us in the Bible. God tells us much of what we need to know right there . . . we just need to read it and do it. The written Word is also important because it does not change. It is clear direction from God. Therefore, any *rhema* word *must* agree with God's revealed will in the Bible. If it is contrary to the Bible in any way . . . it's not from God.

I have known Christians who are strongly attracted to someone of the opposite sex who isn't a Christian. Before too long they begin to feel like

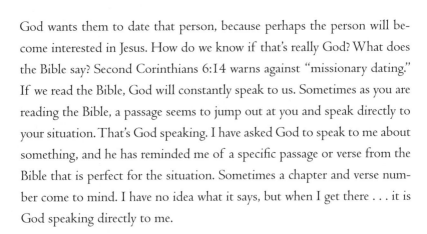

God wants them to date that person, because perhaps the person will become interested in Jesus. How do we know if that's really God? What does the Bible say? Second Corinthians 6:14 warns against "missionary dating." If we read the Bible, God will constantly speak to us. Sometimes as you are reading the Bible, a passage seems to jump out at you and speak directly to your situation. That's God speaking. I have asked God to speak to me about something, and he has reminded me of a specific passage or verse from the Bible that is perfect for the situation. Sometimes a chapter and verse number come to mind. I have no idea what it says, but when I get there . . . it is God speaking directly to me.

3. Look for Confirmation

Mary received this incredible *rhema* word from God, but she held it in her heart until confirmation came through her encounter with Elizabeth. I would have done the same thing. I would want to be very sure before I started broadcasting something like that. This is especially important if it is guidance that we cannot verify with Scripture. Even after Liz's confirmation of what she'd heard, she didn't mention it to Joseph. She waited for God to speak to him directly and confirm through him (Matthew 1:20).

Waiting doesn't mean we are faithless wimps. Being wise does not indicate a lack of faith. Faith is believing what God says, not stepping out in presumption and expecting him to cover us. Confirmation can protect us from false speculation. God does not usually give primary guidance through others. If God wants you to move to India, he will let you know personally. That way you have assurance. Confirmation increases faith and helps double-check our motives (2 Corinthians 13:1).

Often when I hear God's direction I will say nothing about it and wait for confirmation before I mention it to others. Waiting helps us avoid pitfalls like pride or presumption. We need to fully understand what and why God is speaking before we speak out. It also protects us from poor timing;

sometimes we need to discern if it is the right thing and the right time. Confirmation will also protect us from speaking out too early and confusing others when it is not yet solidified in our own minds.

4. What if You're Not Hearing Anything?

God speaks to those who honestly want to hear and *do* what he says. His are not multiple-choice propositions. We need to have an attitude of openness and readiness, agreeing to obey . . . before God speaks. If we are waiting for God to speak before we decide whether we want to do it, we probably won't hear much. We may need to ask ourselves, "Did I do the last thing God told me?" If you are not hearing much from God, go back to the last thing you heard him say . . . have you done that? Sometimes we wonder if we are hearing God, but the real question is, "Are we willing to obey regardless of the cost?" It is kind of like when you are in the middle of playing an intense video game and your mom calls you to dinner. You don't want to be disturbed because you are intensely involved . . . so you pretend you didn't hear.

The more we practice the presence of God, the easier it becomes. It's like recognizing a friend's voice on the phone—the better the acquaintance, the easier it is to recognize him or her. The longer I am married to and live with my wife, the more I can anticipate what she is about to say. Samuel's recognition of God's voice improved as Samuel grew and spent more time with God (I Samuel 3:4-7; 8:7-10; 12:11-18).

God uses a variety of methods of communicating, not to frustrate us, but because it's a relationship. This is the most important thing about communication. We communicate because of the importance of the relationship. It's not only about what God is saying but also the fact that he actually is speaking to us. Communication is the key to a personal relationship. The more God speaks, the more we get to know him . . . and the more we love him.

Making Waves

1. Like Mary, do you feel you are too young or insignificant for God to speak to you? Are you willing to believe that he wants to speak to you?

2. Think of the first time you heard God. What was it like? Describe what happened. How did you know it was God?

3. Do you take time every day just to listen to what God might want to say? Have you given God an opportunity to speak to the situation you are struggling with right now?

4. Do you read the Bible regularly to know God's direction for your life? Could you discern the real deal from the counterfeit?

5. Are you willing to do whatever he asks? If not, why not?

6. Take some time to unload your thoughts, fears and concerns on Jesus. Then wait for God to respond. Be open to different ways he may reply—ready to do what he asks, however odd or stretching it is. Have fun!

List three things God has shown you in this chapter that you don't want to forget.

1.
_____

_____

2.
_____

_____

3.
_____

_____

Be the Wave

Lord, from this moment on I commit to . . .

Spend a few minutes talking to God about how you feel. List some specific prayer points that will help you live out the truths in this chapter.

_____

_____

_____

_____

_____

_____

_____

_____

on a mission for God

John

It was forbidden by order of the state. But in a remote, rural province of southern China, three teenage girls quietly gathered to pray. They assembled in secret, week after week, month after month, to pray for God's move in their province. Then it happened. During an intense time of prayer and crying out to God, he spoke. The girls stopped and excitedly shared their impressions with one another. They each felt exactly the same thing—but it couldn't be right. Was God telling them to go to the villages in their province and preach to whomever would listen? They looked at each other in confusion and bewilderment. How could that be possible? Had they misheard? How could they go and preach? First of all, China is a communist nation. Anyone caught preaching contrary to the official church is imprisoned and punished. Secondly, even if they did go, what would they say? They had no Bible school or missionary training; they had no idea how to preach a sermon. Thirdly, they were girls, and young girls at that. China is a patriarchal society. Women, especially young women, are to be seen and not heard. No one would value the opinion of a teenage girl.

Uncertain and confused, they went back to prayer. But still the word of the Lord was to go. Baffled, they threw their hands up to God as if to question what they were hearing. Finally, they decided they would do what they could—they would be willing and obedient. They would be willing and obedient to do the next thing God told them to do, then the next, then the next. And so they nervously stepped out, with no training, no backing, and no support except the Holy Spirit's lead. Miraculously, after a

little over three months of traveling through the villages in their province, the three teenage girls saw fifty-two new churches established! Three teenage girls—banned from speaking Jesus' name, with no training whatsoever and who, culturally, should not have spoken a single word—witnessed an extraordinary move of God in their province. All because they were willing and obedient—that's all the Lord requires.

John felt a shiver go down his spine as the heavily barred door slammed shut. In resigned hopelessness he leaned back against the cold, stone wall, thumping his head backwards. What would happen to them? He was too young to die. Tears welled up in his eyes as he slid down the wall and crouched in the corner.

"Jesus, I'm afraid," he whispered under his breath.

"We'll be fine, bro," Peter assured him.

But what did Peter know? Jesus wasn't "fine" when he was arrested—he was crucified! The dark, dank, musty smell of the cell began to suffocate him. He pulled his knees to his chest, closed his eyes tightly and thought of home. Peter slid down the wall and sat next to him. "Don't worry, John, it'll just be for tonight; we'll be back with the rest of the guys tomorrow."

John felt his flesh crawl. *Sure*, he thought, *that's if something doesn't eat us first!*

It was the longest night of John's short life. He couldn't sleep. The darkness seemed to swallow time itself. He felt totally alone. His chest tightened. It was hard to breathe. Vivid images danced in his mind. He couldn't find hope for the next day, and it seemed as though the night would last forever. As his heart and mind raced uncontrollably, he could feel the cold, clammy hand of fear slip its fingers around his neck. He was sure he was going to die. The graphic memories of Jesus hanging on the cross blitzed his mind. He heard the wailing of agony. He could almost taste the blood and sweat smeared on Jesus' body, as the stark remembrances pressed against him. He could feel the mud caked to his feet, the

driving rain on his face, the jet-black sky as he looked up at Jesus, covered in blood, naked on the cross. John started to hyperventilate as tears streamed down his face. *Jesus, help me!* he cried out in his mind. Just when he had given up any hope of seeing another sunrise, a rooster announced its arrival. John paced the floor of the putrid cell, partly in nervous anticipation, partly because he was afraid of catching some deadly disease if he sat. He had felt the enemy's attacks before, but this one seemed so real, so true. He couldn't make it on his own. Sobbing, he shook Peter, "Pete, I *need* you to pray!"

It seemed like a massive victory just to be out of the cell alive, even though they were being escorted to the Sanhedrin—the religious supreme court. The heavy bracelets chafed John's wrists until they were red and raw. The immense, ornately carved, wooden doors slowly swung open, and Peter and John were pushed into the middle of a large room. People sitting in tiered seats around three sides of the room surrounded them. The place seemed to explode with uproar as they stumbled in. Lost in the din, John gazed intently into the crowd. Directly in front of him was a special section, separated from all the rest by a low wall. The chairs had cushions and tall straight backs. He recognized Annas, the high priest, and Caiaphas, from the interrogation of Jesus just a few weeks ago. The crowd was called to order as a man spoke loudly with a cynicism that reverberated around the room. "These men are charged with healing a cripple who formerly sat by the Beautiful Gate, by use of unknown supernatural powers . . ."

As the man spoke John felt his body tingle with heat and vibrate with a supernatural boldness. These men were bickering over the love and mercy of God being shown to a poor disabled man? The man, who had been disabled for more than forty years until Peter and John stopped to share Christ's love with him, was standing there with them—still grinning excitedly. Suddenly, Peter's chest puffed up and he exploded. With ferocious boldness he declared their devotion to Jesus. John could feel it too. He waited for Peter

to draw breath so he could release the torrent he felt bubbling within him, but Peter preached on. The crowd sat in silence; even those without cushions were afraid to move a muscle, their faces overwhelmed with astonishment and sheer shock. It was as if John could feel a cosmic force field of truth and authority emanating from his body. Jesus seemed more present, more real to him at that moment, than he had the three years they had lived together. John radiated the presence of his master. A dense silence covered the room like a heavy, wet blanket. Without receiving a word of rebuttal, Peter and John were ordered back to the cell.

Still energized from his preaching, Peter paced the floor. His body surged with adrenaline as he bounced off the walls with a righteous zeal. John simply stood in the corner of the cell and stared at the dust particles floating aimlessly in a shaft of light that streamed in through a small slit high in the wall. They looked so free. As he watched the dust dodge and bump, John's mind slipped back to that fateful day a little over three years ago. A lot had happened since then, but the memories of that day snagged like a splinter in his mind.

John had grown up in a small fishing village called Capernaum on the banks of Galilee. His childhood had been happy though uneventful; his family was well off by most people's standards. His dad owned a fishing company that employed a number of local fishermen. He had hoped to expand to a fleet of vessels, perhaps even franchise, until the Romans put an end to that dream. The taxes and financial penalties made expansion unprofitable. Still, they did quite nicely. John was the youngest (his brother James was a couple of years older), but he had an air about him. For some unknown reason he just attracted people; there was something special about him. His face was full of innocence, although he was nobody's fool. Most of his friends were his brother's age, but he always found himself at the center of a group. Then one crisp morning his entire world was turned on its head, forever.

John stood on the beach, the shallow water lapping at his ankles, preparing the nets for the next day's fishing. He was so engrossed in his work, chatting with some of the men as he grabbed the slimy, salt-stained nets, that he hadn't noticed the approaching figure. He was startled to turn and see Jesus standing on the shore with a couple of other local fishermen. John instantly recognized Simon and Andrew, but who was the stranger with them? He stood on the seashore exuding confidence. There was something about him that drew you to be around him. It was Jesus standing there, all right, but something was different. John couldn't put his finger on what it was, but it was strangely obvious.

The universe seemed to stand still as Jesus stood and looked at the two brothers standing in the shallow water. Finally he broke the silence, "Come on, James . . . it's time." Without a word James handed his ropes to one of the workers next to him and began to walk onto the shore where Jesus stood.

John was riveted; he could not take his eyes off Jesus. The heavens, the earth, the entire cosmos seemed to vanish from existence; all that remained was one man. He stood longing for Jesus to notice him, to speak to him. More than gold or silver he wanted Jesus to notice him. His heart burst in his throat; his body felt as if he had been physically slammed against a wall, and his insides ached as his soul hesitantly, longingly reached out to Jesus. Anxiously John took a half-step forward, reaching his hand out slightly. He wanted to shout after Jesus, but the words felt like concrete. He struggled to find his breath. Jesus feigned turning and walking, then casually turned back. His fiery eyes fixed intently on John as he looked deeply into his soul. "You too, John. Follow me."

John felt a wave of nausea pour over him as he walked away from his father, the fishing business, the only world he had ever known. His head spun. Could this be true? Could this man be the one? They walked in silence for ten, maybe fifteen minutes, and then Jesus began to speak. His words,

though unassuming, seemed to carry the weight of the universe with them; each seemed to pierce and burn deeply into John's heart. The words crashed around his ears, eroding any shred of doubt. Jesus had come to inaugurate the kingdom. He *was* the one. Over the coming weeks and months, John would often stop dead in his tracks and pinch himself to make sure it was real. He felt overwhelmed and stunned, yet inspired and thrilled all at the same time. Jesus, the Messiah, had chosen him—just a young man—to be part of his mission.

For the rest of his life, John would be a youth with a mission, and his goal would be worship. His purpose was to see white-hot worship. As long as there were places and people who did not worship the true God, he would have a mission. Today our mission remains the same, to see white-hot worship fill the nations of the earth. Jesus spoke about the kingdom. He said it was near (Matthew 4:17), upon them (Matthew 12:28), that man must strive to enter it (Matthew 5:20), and he prayed for its arrival (Matthew 6:10). But what did he mean by "the kingdom"? A kingdom may be a geographical realm defined by borders on a map, or it may be the subjects within that realm. But first and foremost it is the authority to rule—the sovereignty of the king.

While hanging on the cross, the thief asked Jesus to remember him when he came into his kingdom—into his rule. Jesus' message was that God's rule was near, that man must choose to enter it and must pray that it happen. To enter the kingdom is to enter into God's sovereign rule. But God is not a tyrannical dictator. His kingdom is the freedom to love and be loved, to run, skip and laugh in the assurance of unconditional love and acceptance. The kingdom is the love relationship with a perfect Father who knows not only what hurts us but also how to heal us. Mother Teresa of Calcutta once said, "What we all want is to be accepted in our broken-ness, affirmed in our weakness, loved in our loneliness. To be relieved of the worst kind of suffering—the feeling of not being accepted or wanted."

The kingdom is what we all long for in our heart of hearts—relief from the exhaustion and weariness of life.

Worship is the front door to the kingdom. Worship is not simply singing songs. In the Bible, *worship* means "to bow the knee." Worship occurs when we say "not my will for my life, but God's"—when we accept God's loving plan for our lives. Worship is not something that happens for thirty minutes before the sermon. It's a lifestyle. John longed to see those bruised and battered by life throw off the shackles of depression and difficulty and enter into perfect freedom and love. As author John Piper says, "Missions exist because worship doesn't." Do you have a mission? John did.

John jumped a little from the shock of feeling Peter's hand on his shoulder, startling him out of his memories and back into the reality of his tiny cell. Peter puffed out his barrel chest and started to sing, loudly. He looked at John, signaling with his crazy eyebrows to join in the chorus. Soon they were marching defiantly around the cramped cell, singing at the tops of their voices and shaking the heavy chains to the beat. "You can take our lives, but you can never take our freedom!" shouted Peter to no one in particular. John sat on a small piece of threadbare sackcloth and propped his back against a wall. Pulling one knee up to his chest, he carefully lifted the heavy iron cuff around his ankle. Lifting the weight brought temporary relief to the raw flesh around his foot. He shifted to the other leg, drawing breath sharply as a stabbing pain shot through his leg. They were both startled as the peepholes on the door were flung open. "Which one of you is John?"

John stood to his feet and shuffled to the door in response. His round, youthful face filled the open area of the door, and he peered into the hall and gazed upon his mom. She was just a few inches away but it felt like an eternity. John longed to hug her. Without thinking he stepped forward, bumping into the heavy cell door. Salome stood in the hallway holding a loaf of fresh

bread. John caught a whiff and his stomach knotted inside him. Bread had never smelled so good; he hadn't eaten since noon the day before.

His mother was dressed in a very smart, formal-looking green robe. The fine stitching and brocade around the sleeves and neck were of a darker shade and made her look very authoritative, almost military. Her thick, slightly graying curls cascaded down from a loosely wrapped scarf that formed a turban on her head. Her favorite yellow-gold earrings seemed tarnished by the dimly lit jail hallway. She was in late middle age, the wife of a successful businessman, but she had a heart that loved God. John had never met anyone as kind and caring as his mom. Many of the young men and women in their town had sat round her kitchen table while she had spoken graceful words of care and advice to them. Over the last few years, she had helped many of them financially, including John.

Her lip quivered as she whispered, fighting back a torrent of tears, "We are all praying and fasting for you."

She forced the bread through the small hole, and for a brief moment her soft, gentle hand rubbed against John's. It was more than she could take. She grabbed his hand as hot tears streamed down her face.

"My baby! Are you OK, son? Oh, how can they do this to you? You're such a good boy—you've always been a good boy." She caught a glimpse of the jailer and turned on him like a rabid animal. "How do you sleep at night? He's just a youth . . . he's a good boy, my John—he wouldn't harm a flea. I don't know how you can live with yourself, locking them up in this tiny, filthy cell! He's a good boy . . ."

The burly jailer looked worried. He backed away and pretended to check on the other cells along the hall. John softly pulled his mother's arm. "It's OK, Mom. It's not his fault. Remember what Jesus said—we have to expect this sort of thing. Anyway, I don't mind, if it gives me an opportunity to witness for him."

Sensing his mother relax just a little, he excitedly grinned from ear to

ear. "Man . . . you should've been there this morning—Pete gave 'em what for!"

"It was awesome, Mrs. Zeb!" shouted Peter from inside the cell. "Hey, tell the peeps hi and keep praying, eh?"

Salome smiled, "Peter, you're incorrigible."

Peter and John waited politely until his mom had gone, then they tore into the bread. "Sweeeet . . . bro," smiled Peter, picking the crumbs out of his thick, black goatee.

"Totally."

The cell was beginning to feel very warm and stuffy as the midday sun shone down on the outer stone wall. John felt his head begin to bob forward as he struggled to stay awake, drifting in and out of consciousness. He kept hearing the words of Jesus over and over in his mind:

Blessed are you when people insult you, persecute you and falsely say all kinds of evil against you because of me. . . . Love your enemies and pray for those who persecute you. **Matthew 5:11, 44**

Blessed to Be a Blessing

Long before John was a twinkle in his mom's eye, God called his ancestor Abram out of his land. In Genesis 12 God promised the man of faith,

---

I will make you into a great nation and I will bless you; I will make your name great, and you will be a blessing. I will bless those who bless you, and whoever curses you I will curse; and all peoples on earth will be blessed through you. **Genesis 12:2, 3**

Understanding this promise is key to understanding our mission. God's

whole strategy is encapsulated in this promise. He chose and called Abram from obscurity in pure grace, not because of what Abram had done. In his grace, God would bless Abram so he could be a blessing to all nations.

It was a twofold strategy. The first aspect is what we call centripetal (toward the center)—others would see God's hand of blessing upon Abram's life and be drawn to God. The second was centrifugal (out from the center)—Abram was to use his resources and abundance to fulfill the mission as he went to the nations. One aspect would draw people into a relationship with God, and the other would challenge them to go out and reach others. Today's descendants of Abram are those who trust in Jesus by faith (Romans 2:28, 29; 9:6-8)—you and me. We have the same mandate. God has blessed us.

Today many of us are abundantly blessed materially and spiritually. We have access to awesome Bible teaching, videos, CDs, music, churches and books galore. You name it. In fact we have such abundance, it all gets a bit blasé and boring. A lot of us have a PC, Xbox®, TV and CD player in our own rooms. Most of us have our own cell phone. Do you know that eight out of nine people in the world don't have any sort of phone? Four out of five have no TV (and no way to watch *American Idol*); eleven out of twelve don't own a PC. More importantly, one in three are hungry. One-third of the world doesn't have safe drinking water, and one in two people has no freedom to express his or her own ideas. What is our response? The annual income of the 1.9 billion professing Christians is $15.2 trillion. The average Christian family makes $34,000 a year (in fact, if you make more than $10,000 a year, you belong to the richest ten percent of people in the world), yet our weekly giving is less than three bucks a week. About fifteen cents goes to missions. We are blessed—but are we blessing or consuming? Jesus is looking for a generation of young people like John, who are white-hot worshipers willing to make the sacrifice and live a less ordinary life. You can change the world, but first you will have to die to self.

Discipling Nations

Abram's mission, our mission, is not just winning souls. It is nothing less than unilateral global redemption. The first step in global redemption is bringing people into a life-changing relationship with Jesus, but it goes beyond that. The truths of God should affect every area of our society, bringing radical transformation. That means we are called to disciple nations and transform worldviews. We are not to divorce ourselves from the world or culture; we are to dive into it and redeem it. John and Peter were hard at that task. They challenged thinking and questioned worldview.

God has given you passions and gifts to redeem all of creation. He wants you to use them. Missions is not necessarily wearing a pith helmet and living in a mud hut in Africa. Many people think that missions means giving up what you love, moving far away from home and being sad most of the time. That couldn't be further from the truth. Missions means embracing your passion and using it to bring white-hot worship to God.

For example, you may have a passion for music. God has given you that desire, that talent, to use it to bring redemption. That gift and desire is from God; he wants you to go for it. God doesn't want to make you do something you don't want to do—it's too much of a headache. You would be grumpy and moaning all the time. He's way smarter than that. He wants to release you in your passion—the thing you have energy for—and see you go for it with all your heart. Use your passion for music to work in the industry and change worldview. Write songs that change worldview and speak of God's precepts. Use your band to open the doors to play in non-Christian colleges and then share the inspiration for your music between songs. Make it your mission. Use your passion and talent for skating to reach a whole subculture. Start a Christian skateboard or surfboard design company . . . whatever. Dream big dreams and follow your passion. Go into all spheres of society with the mission of redeeming cultures and discipling nations.

In England in the nineteenth century, there was a Christian who wanted to disciple a nation. He's famous for riding his horse all over the country and preaching the gospel in pubs, on the streets and outside factories as workers came in and out. He preached at least five times a day, his first sermon beginning at 5:00 AM! Thousands were saved, and a revival broke out in the nation.

But this man did a lot more than just preach. He opened the first free medical clinics and wrote medical and grammar books. He campaigned against bribery and corruption, and he began a movement that led to fair wages and employment for all. He fought for changes in prisons, founded microeconomic enterprise and vocational training for the unemployed. Through his tireless campaign and his influence upon a politician named William Wilberforce, slavery in England was abolished. The groundswell he started led to the founding of organizations like the YMCA, the Salvation Army, the Society for the Protection of Cruelty Against Animals, the Boy Scouts, Girl Guides, Barnardo's children's homes . . . the list is endless. He was a freak! He burned for white-hot worship, and he discipled a nation. His name was John Wesley. Your generation is a Wesley generation. You have the potential to do even greater things. Will you dare to dream?

Without warning the heavy cell door swung open as the jailer boomed, "All right, you two, let's go!"

The Sanhedrin was still buzzing with conversation—some of it heated— as Peter and John were led back in. The healed man was still there, but now he sat in the corner looking exhausted from the interrogation. He appeared completely bewildered and browbeaten; his body language seemed to shout, "I've been set free. Why can't you just be happy?"

Annas leaned forward in his cushioned chair. He swiveled to set his cup of wine onto the side table, and then looking back at John, he threatened them if they ever mentioned Jesus' name again. His beady eyes spat venom

and disdain at John as he promised that any further spreading of these "lies" would cost them their lives next time.

For a split second Pete and John looked at each other. Was this it? If they obeyed it would all be over. The last three years would mean nothing. The cross would be forgotten—the resurrection a fading memory soon to disappear from remembrance altogether. If they never spoke of Jesus again, the church and Christianity itself would come to a grinding halt, dry up and disappear from history as fast as it came. With one eye still fixed on Peter, John spoke with a thundering voice, "We can't help telling people about what we have seen and heard. No threat, no bribe, no force in this world or the one to come can stop us from claiming our inheritance. We will not go silently into the night!"

Annas flew into a rage, spouting threats of hideous punishment and torture. "Get them out of my sight!" he roared.

Eternal Inheritance

John and Peter would not give up their destiny, their inheritance in the kingdom. Will we? God has an eternal inheritance for us if we will dare to claim it. He has the adventure of a lifetime for us as we abandon everything in pursuit of the only thing that really matters. No other group in the history of the universe is more important or central than the group that embraces their mission and proclaims the kingdom with their lives. The destiny of modern civilization, and of human history, hangs on your response. You are more important than presidents or prime ministers. Your response is more significant and more important than White House policy or United Nations mandates. The divine purpose of global history is accomplished in the fulfillment of our mission. What you do matters! It has eternal significance. The destiny of history is in your hands. What will you do with it?

Or will we choose to forfeit our inheritance for stuff that rusts and rots? Will we sell out for something cheap—a flashy car with leather seats

and power windows, a house or salaries that will make us feel important? I don't know about you, but I don't want to give up my God-given right, my destiny—my inheritance—for something as cheap as a BMW, or a comfy armchair. I want the nations as my inheritance, the kingdom as my reward.

Follow Me?

How do we know whether Jesus is calling us into the mission? Well, if you're a Christian, you're called and qualified. Remember, the mission is using your passion and gifting to see God's kingdom come. That may mean leaving home and living in a foreign culture to see white-hot worship established. It may mean using your talents right where you are. You may be called to Afghanistan or you may be called to advertising—they are both mission fields.

Still not sure that you're called? Here is a foolproof test. Open your Bible to Matthew 28:18-20. Does your Bible have these verses? OK, check Mark 16:15. Got it? Then you are called. If you are a follower of Jesus, he has called you to the mission—to *go*. To *go* into all the world—every nation, every sphere of society—and see white-hot worship established. You don't need to pray *whether* you should go, but rather *where* and *how*. Here are some ideas for getting started.

- *Pray about going on a short-term mission trip.*
- *Get involved in something locally.*
- *Start a white-hot worship group with some friends. Commit to pray for God's kingdom and do whatever God asks to see it established.*

I guarantee you this—if you dare to live life on the edge and follow hard after Jesus to see his kingdom come, it will be the greatest adventure of your life.

John continued to embrace the mission to see white-hot worship. Within days he stood once again before the Sanhedrin. Annas fumed with anger,

his veins popping on his burning, red face. John and his friends were beaten severely until they thought life would ebb out of their broken and bruised bodies. Then they were warned, once again, never to mention Jesus. The Bible says that they left that day "rejoicing because they had been counted worthy of suffering disgrace for the Name" (Acts 5:41).

Before his death, many years later, John would see white-hot worship spread across many nations. He claimed his inheritance. He would not trade it for any worldly trinket. How about us? The mission awaits fulfillment. We can make it happen if we will be youth with a mission.

Making Waves

----

1. Spend some time praying and asking God for your mission. What is he saying?

----

2. Are you willing to go anywhere and do anything?

----

3. Are there areas in your life in which you are not worshiping God? List any areas or actions in which your will has not bowed to God's. Will you bow your will to his?

----

4. What are your passions, your interests? How could you use them to see God's kingdom come? Think big.

----

5. How has God blessed you? How can you use your blessing to bless others? Be specific and follow through.

----

6. What will you sacrifice to see white-hot worship?

----

7. What are you investing in the mission? Money? Time?

----

8. Is your own worldview Bible-based? How can you change it? How can you impact your society and change its worldview?

List three things God has shown you in this chapter that you don't want to forget.

1.

2.

3.

Be the Wave

Lord, from this moment on I commit to . . .

Spend a few minutes talking to God about how you feel. List some specific prayer points that will help you live out the truths in this chapter.

intimacy with God

Mary of Bethany

"If you come here again, we will beat you!"

Raj was surrounded. A motley bunch of militant Hindus pushed and prodded his chest with their bony fingers, intent on intimidating him. This was Raj's first day in the small fishing community nestled on a polluted beach outside of Chennai, India. Raj had followed the call of God and moved with his wife from their village to the big city of Chennai. He had felt God drawing his heart to a small, very poor community of people that were mostly ignored by the rest of society—the local fishermen. His strategy was to serve the community by meeting the needs of its children. Few of these kids ever went to school. Scraping through each day takes so much energy that the youngest children are left to wander the streets until they are old enough to help with the chores. Raj wanted to start a preschool, where he would teach, feed, clothe and care for the children.

The village was very poor. The families lived on the beach in small, shanty-style hovels made of cardboard, tin and rubbish. Each house leaned up against the next like a drunk desperately clinging to a lamppost before passing out. There was no electricity, running water or sewer, and raw sewage littered the beach. Disease was rampant.

From the shore, Raj could watch the men bobbing up and down in their little wooden boats as they threw the nets into the shallow ocean waters and dragged them back up. The women were also hard at work, boiling their small measures of rice, washing a few threadbare clothes or hunting for plastic and trash that could be used or traded. Naked babies

clung to their busy mothers or sat unattended in the crusty sand as stray dogs sniffed around, looking for scraps. Raj walked slowly through the passageways between the shanty houses, pausing here and there to tell his plan to whomever would listen.

Suddenly, he found himself surrounded by a gang of greasy, dirty, vicious-looking young men. They pushed Raj around the circle, shouting and threatening him. The gang leader thrust his hands onto Raj's shoulders and sent him reeling into the group behind him. He was sweaty and stank of cigarettes and cheap liquor; his shirt was undone, exposing a scar on his otherwise smooth, dark chest. "We know why you are here. If you speak about your Jesus here, we will beat you!"

Raj, slightly doubled over, looked up and sideways at the man. His shoulders still stung from the blow. "Is that all you can do?" he asked, politely yet defiantly.

The entire group jumped on Raj and began to hit and kick him without mercy. He felt the sharp blows rain down all over his body and head. As he fell to the ground, the thugs began to kick him in the stomach and kidneys. A sharp, electrifying stab of pain shot through his torso as one of his ribs broke. His chin was covered in the blood that gushed out of his mouth as he gasped for breath.

"Come back again and we will kill you!" shouted the gang leader as he wiped the sweat from his top lip with the back of his hand.

"I will come back. Jesus has asked me to come here," spluttered Raj. Everything spun wildly around, and he felt overwhelmed with nausea as a kick to the face sent his head snapping back. Then all went blank.

Raj spent the next few days recovering in bed. As soon as he felt strong enough, he went back to the fishing village. Over the next months he was beaten and threatened repeatedly, but he faithfully began reaching out to the families and their children. Then one afternoon as the gang surrounded him, a large group of fishermen sprang out as if from nowhere.

"You leave this man alone," said one of the fishermen to the gang. "He loves our children and our community—we will protect him."

The gang, seriously outnumbered, huffed, puffed, threatened and then slithered away. From that day on they kept a close eye on Raj, but they didn't dare touch him again. Many of those fishermen and their families are now Christians. Things are changing in the community, and Raj has reached out to another fishing village where he has been able to plant a church. Raj lived out of an intimacy with Jesus. He knew Jesus' heart and shared it with a disdained, disregarded people who needed to know the gentle touch of a gracious Father.

Jesus looked fondly around the room. He loved fellowship like this. He particularly loved anywhere there was going to be good food and drink. He was the life of the party and was not going to miss this. He felt content to gaze around the room as people laughed and chatted softly. The balmy room glowed golden as the flickering flame of the oil lamps danced on the walls. He looked over to the corner of the room, and a smile played on the corners of his mouth as he noticed Peter, who was deep in intense discussion. Without noticing his admirer, Peter frowned, then suddenly exploded into loud laughter, spilling his drink everywhere.

Jesus laughed to himself as he remembered the look of sheer confusion that had been on Peter's face the day he told him to feed 5,000 men with just a few loaves of bread. It was priceless. Or the frustration John had vented at not understanding the meaning of a parable—even on its fifth explanation. The other disciples had been relentless with John that night, teasing him until he jumped to his feet and promised them all a good thrashing—including Jesus, who was howling with laughter.

Time seemed to stand still inside the room that evening. It was so warm and inviting that Jesus sighed, wishing it would never end. He soaked up the sheer joy of every second as he stared deeply into the eyes of his dear friends. He looked at young Mary, the sister of Lazarus and Martha. Sipping on his wine he thought of the day he had met this passionate young woman.

Jesus had been invited to speak at a midweek Bible study that met in a house in Bethany on the Mount of Olives, in the outskirts of Jerusalem. It was a warm, humid evening as they made their way up the chalky hill from Jericho. They ambled along the small streets of the town, pausing at a well for a cool, refreshing drink of water. James grinned slyly at Andy, then doused him with the sparkling, clear, but very chilly well water. Suddenly all-out war broke loose, as the thirteen became embroiled in a furious water fight. Minutes later they collapsed on the muddy ground and propped themselves against a wall, laughing uncontrollably. Jesus sprang up and began to inspect a fig tree; he threw a fig over to Philip. "Taste that!"

The sky was a deep burnt-orange as they arrived at the address. A chilly evening breeze picked up as they were ushered into a large rambling house. Peter whistled as he kicked off his sandals, "Are we in the right place?" They filed into a large, comfortable room with gleaming tile floors and furniture with big, plump cushions.

"Wow, this is what I'm talkin' about. This is my kinda pad," emphasized Peter.

A small group of people had already gathered and sat around the room. The disciples made eye contact with the regulars in the group and awkwardly greeted them. They felt a bit uncomfortable, but they seemed to be with a new group of strangers every other night, so they were getting used to it. A young man with a paisley headband tied round his head (to keep his long, curly hair out of his face) casually greeted the group and began to play music on his guitar softly. Soon the group was lost in worship as they sang choruses and psalms. The room filled with a sense of awe and hushed worship. As the music faded away, people around the room were lost in worship. Some were kneeling with hands lifted to the heavens

expectantly. Others sat quietly weeping and praising God.

Crash! Bang! A clattering, clanging noise violated the beauty of the moment. Everyone in the room looked around, obviously disturbed. Where was that insensitive disturbance coming from? The hippie worship leader looked sheepish and tried to distract the crowd.

"We have a very special speaker tonight who originally comes from Galilee."

He paused, then with a look of embarrassment leaned forward and asked Andrew, "Which of you is it?" Jesus looked very much at home with the quirky little group. He always did. He smiled and made a funny comment about the trip, which put everyone at ease. He always seemed to know just what to say and how to say it.

Bang! Splash! Everyone jumped as the strange noise invaded the room again.

"What is that?" asked James impatiently.

"Oh . . . please go on, Jesus, um . . . you were saying?" Again the worship leader nervously tried to ignore the distraction.

Undisturbed, Jesus picked his sentence back up and continued. "For the kingdom of heaven is like a landowner who went out early in the morning to hire men to work in his vineyard. . . ."

The disciples smiled at each other smugly and nudged one another in the ribs, nodding knowingly. Jesus had told this tale once or twice before, but it was worth hearing again. They loved the ending—it was so controversial. Jesus, as usual, would get everybody lulled into the story, thinking they knew exactly where it was going; then he would twist it around and speak of the Father's amazing goodness and grace. As he unfolded the story, he noticed young Mary jump from her seat on the other side of the room and eagerly sit cross-legged on the floor right in front of him. Mary was the youngest of three who lived in the sprawling house that played host to the home group. A bright-eyed and carefree young woman, she loved

hanging out and talking with friends. Her sister called her a slacker, but she just had different ideas about life—to her, relationships were more important than tasks. The way she figured, careers, achievements or possessions would all fade eventually—relationships were the only thing that could last. She believed that spending time with a person could be more important than doing things for them.

As the story progressed Mary's eyes got wider and wider as she hung on Jesus' every word. She inched forward until she was almost sitting on his feet. She was so enthralled she didn't seem to notice the loud, unmistakable crash of a large cooking pot.

"What the . . . ?"

"It's coming from the kitchen," someone said.

The worship leader looked as if he was about to bail.

Before anyone could say another word, a red-faced, flustered woman peered around the wall from the kitchen. Her forehead was covered with sweat and lined with a large white stripe where she had wiped away the sweat with flour-covered hands. She had the sort of look that would make a WWE wrestler turn tail and run for his mommy. No one in the room dared breathe, afraid that she would give them such a look that they would spontaneously combust. With a glare of righteous indignation, she faced Jesus and grabbed the top of her apron with both hands, like a lawyer ready to interrogate her witness.

"Don't you care that Mary has left me to do *all* the work by myself?"

The worship leader headed for the bathroom.

Everyone fidgeted in the room uneasily. One man looked at his watch; most looked at their feet. Tom looked glad he wasn't in charge.

"Why is it that all you do-gooders sit around and talk a good game, but then never lift a finger to help anyone? How about telling her to give me a hand?" Martha continued.

If Jesus was intimidated, he hid it well. He simply looked Martha square in the eyes and said firmly, "You are worried and upset about all sorts of stuff, when only one thing is really important. Mary has chosen what is better, and it won't be taken from her."

Mary pursued intimacy with Jesus. Intimacy with him is like sinking into a big, overstuffed, comfy chair when you're really tired. You sink down, relax and let everything go, as the acceptance of God's love engulfs and supports you. You feel completely relaxed and rested. All the cares and stress, the aches and pains, melt away. Anyone watching would see the effect on you; it's obvious. Mary was obvious. She had a touch of innocence, pure love of life and a goofy grin. She had a peace in her very core, as if she had slipped into the ancient rhythms of God's grace. Intimacy is taking time to hang out with Jesus, to be still with him, to listen and wait. The only focus is to reach out and touch his heart. If we can reach out and touch God's heart, it will be enough—we will be changed. Jesus said this is the best thing we can do—it's what he desires.

Life with Jesus is not about stuff, what we can do or accomplish. Christianity is not a list of do's and don'ts—it's wild, ferocious love. It's an intimate love relationship—a place where we don't feel embarrassed or ashamed before Jesus, where we trust his love and acceptance, where we can get honest in an atmosphere of grace and safety. It's much easier to just *do* things, follow rules or look busy—but it's not what Jesus longs for. Quiet your heart and pursue the best. Here are some pointers from Mary's life.

1. Accept Yourself as Jesus Does

There was a time when people of various colorful backgrounds were coming to Jesus with the childlike hope of acceptance. Some of the squeaky-clean religious people saw it and clucked their tongues in disapproval. So Jesus released a trilogy. In episode one, Jesus told of a shepherd who left ninety-nine sheep to set off in search of one lost little lamb.

Episode two featured a woman who turned her house upside down looking for a lost coin. The final installment featured a young man who demanded his inheritance and took off in search of the good life. I'm sure you know the story of the Prodigal Son in Luke 15. In the middle of the story is this famous line:

But while he was still a long way off, his father saw him and was filled with compassion for him; he ran to his son, threw his arms around him and kissed him. **Luke 15:20**

I always imagined the father standing on his front porch each morning, coffee in hand, scouring the horizon and thinking, "Oh, my son, where are you?" But then I realized the theme of Jesus' trilogy is "The Search." The shepherd searched for the sheep, the woman turned the house upside down and the father pursued his son. The father didn't stand on the porch and pine for his son—he abandoned the farm and took off, searching through the towns and villages for his beloved son. He had to—he couldn't help himself. Then, in the midst of his search, he saw his beloved child. He didn't care the slightest what anybody thought or said about him; he ran with reckless abandon to his son, tears streaming down his face. He fell on his neck and kissed him all over like the crazy lovesick parent he was. There were no lectures, no "I told you so's" and no guilt trips. He just wanted to be with the son he loved.

Mary trusted that Jesus would give her the same welcome. Perhaps, because of death or divorce, you haven't experienced intimacy with a parent. Like many, you may have been "orphaned" by the demands of careers on your parents. With disappointments like these, it's hard to see God as caring or as willing to take time to be with you, to listen to you, to just be quiet and hear the sound of two hearts becoming one. It's hard to forget

the broken promises of childhood and believe that God will be different. But God has always been there, every second, every moment. When you were sick and lay awake all night, he lay with you. When you felt the sting of rejection from a friend, he wept with you. When you felt alone and abandoned, he held your hand.

Mary dared to believe and found acceptance. Jesus loved hanging out with her. She was an awkward, geeky, young woman—but Jesus loved her company and even asked where she was when she wasn't around (John 11:28). Imagine how that made Mary feel! Jesus valued her more than what she could do for him; he valued her more than things. We grow up hearing how valuable *things* are—cars, money, time—more than we hear how valuable *we* are. Stuff can seem more important than we are. God values us more than any amount of stuff.

You captivate the Father. He loves to sit at the end of your bed and watch you while you sleep, anxiously waiting for that moment when your sleepy eyes will flutter open. Like a proud parent, he flicks through the memory album of his mind, cherishing every moment, every event. Remember your first boyfriend or girlfriend? How you thought about him or her constantly and wrote his or her name all over your notebook? (Come on, you know you did!) God is just like that. He can't get you off his mind. His love is unconditional—there is nothing you can do to earn it or lose it. Jesus just loves being with you. He never rejects, never postpones, never forgets and never tells you he's too tired to spend time with you.

2. Give Yourself a Break

No doubt you are familiar with the WWJD phenomenon, but have you ever asked yourself, "What Would Jesus *Say?*" What would he say to us as we sheepishly look up, holding the chipped pieces of our lives like a broken toy? Do you expect him to chide or correct? Do you anticipate a lecture and a spanking, or one of those "I am very disappointed with you, you've

let me down—I expect better from you next time" guilt-trip speeches? I think Jesus would say something more like:

"It's OK. Lighten up—and go easy on yourself."

"Smile—don't take yourself so seriously."

"Enjoy life—worry less."

"Don't worry about that—come and play!"

We know how much God loves us, and we have put our trust in him. God is love, and all who live in love live in God, and God lives in them. And as we live in God, our love grows more perfect. So we will not be afraid on the day of judgment, but we can face him with confidence because we are like Christ here in this world. 1 John 4:16, 17, NLT

The apostle John, who wrote those verses, knew that Jesus longs to free us from the guilt we create in his name so we can lighten up on ourselves. Assurance of God's love allows us to drop our defenses of performance or indifference and dare to dream, to realize our cracks and chips . . . and smile anyway. It's OK to have cracks and chips—we don't have to be perfect or cover them up by trying harder. Don't take yourself so seriously. Take a look at the sort of people Jesus loved hanging out with:

- A dishonest tax collector so overcome with his moral degradation that it drove him up a tree!
- A blind man who would not quit bugging Jesus.
- A single mom, not too proud to ask for help with the kids.
- A woman of questionable character who threw herself at Jesus.
- A ragtag group of ordinary guys who constantly messed up and failed to show any amount of faith or grace, time after time, and who abandoned him in his hour of need.
- The lost, broken, chipped, cracked, burned-out dropouts. The

desperate, who felt life was just out of their control.

People just like you and me.

I'm no one exceptional or special. I'm not a great leader. I don't have it all together. To be honest, I'm a bit of a mess. I'm a simple clay pot that's chipped and cracked; the paint is peeling in places. I have spiritual scabs all over my knees and elbows where I keep falling down. I struggle with acceptance and pride. I want to do something great but am afraid I never will. I don't feel particularly gifted. I feel very average.

But my Father is nuts about me!

Daring to believe his wild, furious love fills me with the hope that I am special and I can embrace his dreams for my life. Our Father is crazy with love and delight for us.

3. Just Be Yourself, Be Open and Honest With God

We often lack intimacy with God because of a misperception of him. We struggle to feel worthy of his presence, so we pretend to be something we're not. We believe there is some unwritten rule about having to pretend in our relationships. So we act as if everything is fine and dandy, when really we are silently struggling and feel desperately lonely. Pretense is the accepted norm in modern relationships—no one is really honest. But people who pretend have pretend relationships. God desires authenticity.

He wants you to be honest and open with him. It's OK; he can handle it! Share the areas of disappointment, hurt and fear with him. He knows anyway. There is no deep, dark secret, no horrible revelation that you are going to share with him that will turn him off. He isn't intimidated by our honesty—he loves it. He won't ever say, "Oh, I wasn't expecting that—that changes everything" or "That's more than I can handle."

In fact, until we are honest with God, he can't help us. You can't help someone who won't admit they have a problem. In Psalm 13, David honestly tells God exactly how he feels. He feels forgotten, abandoned in his

time of need. He feels God has hidden from him as he wrestles with deep sorrow. He shouts out, "Answer me!" God responds to his honest cry, and the psalm ends with David trusting God's unfailing love and singing worship songs. That's intimacy. That's what we all secretly long for.

Intimacy is the assurance that God is approachable. Jesus not only welcomes us to come, he came to us. Tell God how you really feel. He loves that.

4. Relax and Smile

Spending time with God isn't just about interceding during national crises, praying for your grandma or repenting. You can hang out with God in the same way as with your friends. Listen to music with him, watch TV or read together. God even likes to hang out at the mall. Intimacy is an attitude that will affect our actions. Be warned—spending time hanging out with God may fill us with a thrilling awareness that God loves us unconditionally, just as we are—not as we should be. This awareness can liberate us from a boring, sterile existence and move us into a wild, extravagant love affair. Mahatma Gandhi once said, "I love your Christ—it's Christians I don't like, because they are so unlike Christ." Are we wild lovers of life? Are we accepting, generous and forgiving? Are we intoxicating and wacky? Are we fun to hang out with? Or are we more like Martha—going through the motions and wanting to make everyone else just as miserable as we are?

One thing is for sure: Jesus was never a bore. In fact he was so exciting, so vibrant, so dynamic, so full of life, that he was deemed to be unsafe for human consumption. Jesus needed a warning label: "Caution! May cause you to bust out of your stiff, stuffy, devaluing mindset and get all crazy. Has been known to result in laughing and general goofiness!"

Jesus reached for the jug to refill his empty glass. He had only a few days of this life left to live, but what better place was there to spend his final evenings than with his friends? Could they have any idea how different

things would be in less than a week? Jesus tried to shrug off the thoughts of tomorrow. Mary still didn't say much, but her face lit up every time Jesus was around. He loved that; it made him feel special and wanted.

Suddenly Mary became aware of her admirer's gaze and shot Jesus a puzzled look as if to say "What?" Jesus stared back blankly, then screwed his face up, dropped his jaw and stuck out his tongue to make his best funny face. Mary giggled softly and shook her head. As they stared Mary's smile slowly evaporated. She looked perplexed, then sullen. She covered her mouth with her fingers, and her face flushed as a single tear rolled down her cheek. She sprang up and ran out of the room to keep everyone from seeing the torrent of tears on the verge of breaking through. Jesus was about to follow her when Simon plopped down onto the pillow next to him and launched into conversation. Jesus tried to focus, but his mind was worried about Mary.

For a few minutes the rest of the room continued to hum with conversation. No one had noticed anything. Then suddenly Mary burst back into the room, and this time she wasn't holding anything back. Her face was awash with tears, her eyes already puffy and red. Guests looked disgruntled by the emotional disturbance. Their disapproving looks shouted at her to calm down and stop spoiling the fun. Mary paid no attention to the looks or complaints as she pushed past everyone and over their outstretched legs. She lunged headlong and landed at Jesus' well-tanned feet. Reflex caused Jesus to immediately pull his feet, but Mary grabbed them firmly and gently pulled them back toward herself. Jesus relaxed and submitted. From the folds of her robe, Mary produced a small, dark, ornately carved container. It was made of alabaster and looked very expensive. With a flick of her wrist, she broke the tight seal, and an exquisite floral scent wafted through the room, filling every corner with its exotic yet unmistakable aroma.

But why was Mary pouring nard over Jesus' feet? Nard was for anointing dead bodies, and it was very, very expensive. What on earth was she

doing? As Mary emptied the jar onto his feet and head, people started to grumble. The smell was overpowering as the thick liquid ran off his feet and dribbled to the floor. Without looking up, Mary continued gently massaging the oil into his feet. This was a ridiculous waste. Something had to be said.

"Why on earth are you wasting this precious perfume, you silly girl? That's worth a small fortune—do you have any idea how many poor people that could have fed?"

Someone in the room commented on how youth is wasted on the young.

Jesus was offended, too, but not at the extravagance of Mary. Jesus leaned forward and took Mary's face in his hands. With his thumbs he gently wiped aside her tears and looked into her nervous eyes. "Leave her alone," he said to her accusers. "Why are you bothering her? She has done a beautiful thing to me . . ."

No one had a clue what Jesus meant. Judas was so offended he indignantly walked out and took matters into his own hands by negotiating Jesus' arrest.

Intimacy with Jesus leads to the heart of God. Mary developed intimacy with Jesus, and her heartbeat began to resonate with the rhythms of grace. As we take time to be still, pursuing intimacy and honesty, we develop friendship with the Father—and his friends know his heart (John 15:15). A master tells his servant what to do without explanation. He expects obedience without information. As the relationship develops, the Father loves to share the things that burden his heart. God knew he could entrust the heavy things of his heart to Mary. He trusted the friendship that had been forged in intimacy. She was the only person the Father could entrust his heart to as he shared the burden that Jesus carried before his crucifixion.

Mary was so close to the Father's heart that no gift was too great.

Without a second thought she took the most valuable thing she had and poured it out for Jesus. Servants will fulfill only what is absolutely required. Lovers go above and beyond, giving anything and everything to their loved ones. What everyone else in the room saw as a waste, Jesus recognized as the gift of his beloved.

As Mary developed intimacy her ministry focus shifted. Servants minister *for* Jesus, intimate friends minister *to* Jesus. Everyone in the room thought about using the nard to minister in Jesus' name, but Mary used the nard to minister to Jesus. Lovers are intent on blessing the heart of their beloved. As we develop intimacy and reach out to touch the heart of God, we will be changed as well.

Making Waves

----

1. Has your Christian walk been more about *doing* or *being?*

----

2. Over the last few months have you acted more like a Mary or a Martha? Why?

----

3. Do you struggle to believe that God is infatuated with you and longs just to be with you? Why? Read what God thinks about you in Song of Songs 4:7-15.

----

4. If you feel lost, are you willing to let God find you?

----

5. Does your relationship with your parents help or hinder your trust of the Father? Is there anyone you can talk to about it?

----

6. What do you think Jesus would say to you? Look how he responded to the people in Mark 10:46-52; Luke 5:12, 13; 7:36-50 and John 8:1-11.

----

7. Is there anything you need to get honest with God about? Will you do it?

----

8. Have you been ministering *for* Jesus or *to* him?

----

9. Are you willing to give anything and everything to God? Is there anything he is asking for that you don't want to let go of? Why?

List three things God has shown you in this chapter that you don't want to forget.

1. _____

_____

2. _____

_____

3. _____

_____

Be the Wave

Lord, from this moment on I commit to . . .

Spend a few minutes talking to God about how you feel. List some specific prayer points that will help you live out the truths in this chapter.

_____

_____

_____

_____

_____

_____

_____

_____

_____

Chapter ten

death to self

Timothy

Cars flashed past as my old, red station wagon spluttered along in the slow lane of a fast-moving autobahn in the middle of Germany. I rolled the radio knob in my fingers, straining my ears for anything sounding remotely English. With a German vocabulary limited to words like *bratwurst* and *achtung baby,* finding something I recognized was a hard task. My ears pricked up when I heard the word *Colorado.* It was of particular interest not just because it was the first word I had understood in the last 150 miles, but also because I had just moved from Denver. I listened intently, making small, precise adjustments of the tuning, thinking that if I got it just right, it might sound more English. All I could tell was that an obvious tragedy had occurred. It was April 20, 1999. The shot that rang around the world that day came from Columbine High School. As I struggled to pick out familiar words, it all seemed distant, like it had occurred on another planet.

Later that year I was in Texas, at my in-laws' home. It was a Wednesday evening. The phone rang. A friend was calling us on his cell phone as he drove past Wedgwood Baptist Church, less than a quarter of a mile from where we were sitting. A young man had just walked into the youth service, fired several shots and then turned the gun on himself. This was not a distant event—it was in our own backyard. We had friends at that church.

There has never been so much opportunity for prosperity, so why is our society destroying itself? No generation has ever known the pressures that surround you today. Materialism, education, drugs, sex, guns, gangs, alcohol, a drive to be the best and richest and most successful . . . the stress is crushing. In a world where moral absolutes are no longer assured, how do we know right from wrong? How can we have pure passion and make a difference in a world that faces such overwhelming problems?

Timothy's home life in Lystra (modern-day Turkey) was dysfunctional and tumultuous. His family was a strange mix of culture and belief with a Jewish mom and a Greek dad. As a Jew, it would have been inappropriate for his mother to marry a Gentile (a non-Jew), so she must not have taken her faith seriously at the time. Then sometime after she was married, perhaps while Tim was still a young kid, she became a Christian. The house suddenly flexed with tension. His mom and dad now disagreed about everything. His father felt betrayed and resented the "cult" that had brainwashed her. He was angry and felt cheated. Why had she changed? This was not the woman he had married. The different values created a rift between them like the Grand Canyon. His father withdrew into a secular lifestyle. His mom only seemed interested in being at the church whenever the doors were open. Tim had to take sides constantly, choosing between church with mom or fishing with dad. Either way he would alienate one of them. An underlying tension permeated every meal as Dad made fun of Mom for following a dead man. Was she so weak she needed a crutch? It was all a big con, or worse, a cult. He resented her for taking their child and filling his head with such rubbish.

The more Tim's mother tried to reach his dad, the more she alienated him, until finally one day his mom broke the news, "Tim, your dad is moving out; he won't be living with us anymore."

Tim felt awash with nausea. It was like someone had just punched him in the gut. His head was spinning—he felt crushed. He felt abandoned. His mind was swirling with confusing thoughts. Didn't his dad love him? What had Tim done wrong? He felt responsible. What should he have done to be a better son, not to have driven his dad away? The rejection and loss filled his heart. At school the kids made fun of his mother, the "weird do-gooder." Tim's childhood was awkward. He was the only church kid in his class at school. He wasn't allowed to do most of the stuff the other kids did. He didn't have a dad to play in the yard with or teach him all the guy stuff. He loved his mom, but it was hard not having his dad around. Tim spent most evenings at the back of the church or in some home group meeting or other. He would do his schoolwork in the hall, or sometimes there would be one or two other kids to play with.

Timothy struggled with many of the same pressures we know today, but he found peace in his relationship with God. God became his best friend and the Father he missed. Many nights Tim would go to bed early and lie in his room, dreaming of being on some great adventure with God. In some mysterious way, he was aware of God's love and acceptance. He was somehow sure God would not leave him. When he got a little older, he dedicated his life to being a true disciple. By the time the apostle Paul showed up at Tim's church, everyone told him about the young man. Tim liked Paul, though he was a little intimidated by his hard looks and stern preaching. But he longed to be accepted by Paul, and he tried extra hard to earn his approval. He knew Paul would be leaving soon, but he wasn't prepared for what happened next. At first he thought he was in trouble. Why would such an important man like Paul want to speak with him? Had he done something wrong? He sat timidly in the hard, wooden chair, not daring to look the great apostle in the eye. Paul thoughtfully stroked his beard and then calmly inquired, "Tim, would you like to come with me?"

Tim's jaw dropped, and a dumbfounded look spread across his young face. "Would I like to come with you . . . are you kidding?"

After all these years Tim would find a father in the form of this single-minded preacher. Paul would pour his life into Tim, who would soon become the son Paul had never had.

Tim's mom burst into tears as he hugged her good-bye outside their

little home. She kept saying how proud she was and how happy for him, but he knew she would miss him very much. A single tear rolled down the face of his grandmother as she held his hands and looked deeply into his face. Granny had been living with them for a few years now. Tim thought back over those years; his granny had taught him so much about prayer and intimacy with God. She had such a peace; it was almost like being with Jesus. Tim fumbled for words, "I'm going to miss . . ."

His granny quietly but firmly cut him off mid-sentence, "God has a destiny, a purpose for you. It's going to be amazing—don't look back." She always knew just what to say.

Tim struggled to keep up with Paul's fast pace as they walked out of town. He doubled his step as Paul told Tim what it meant to be a disciple. The term *disciple* came about long before Paul and Timothy. Before there were kindergartens, prep schools, high schools or universities, a young person would learn about life, morals and work from his parents. A young boy would hang out almost exclusively with his dad. From a young age he would learn guy stuff like how to grunt or how to throw that perfect spiral. He would also learn his father's trade. Jesus was a carpenter because his earthly father, Joe, was a carpenter. Jesus learned the trade by doing it with his father, and he learned to do it exactly like his father. He would learn the same technique with the same unusual habits and nuances. If Joseph held the shaft of the ax with his left hand, that's how Jesus would have learned. If Joe had a ritual of spitting on his hands before lifting the ax, Jesus would do the same thing. He became an exact representation.

Being a disciple takes commitment and hard work. Paul warned Timothy he would have to train hard.

Train yourself to be godly. For physical training is of some value, but godliness has value for all things, holding promise for both the present life and the life to come. **1 Timothy 4:7, 8**

When I was in school, I was a fine-tuned machine, the pinnacle of athletic conditioning. Today the machine needs a serious overhaul. While I would love to look like the beautiful people on TV who have sculpted, bronzed bodies and wear nothing but a pair of cool Hawaiian shorts, I look more like an albino Barney in Speedo® swim trunks! You know why I don't look like the guys on *The O.C.?* It's hard work. The transformation from Homer Simpson to a chiseled Adonis takes discipline. The word *discipline* comes from the word *disciple.* Disciples of Jesus are people who have disciplined themselves to live godly lives. Greg Laurie, senior pastor of Harvest Christian Fellowship in Riverside, California, has said, "Every disciple is a follower, but not every follower is a disciple." A disciple of Jesus is someone who has spent so much time in his presence—learning from him, influenced by him—that he begins to have the same lifestyle. Jesus said,

Everyone who is fully trained will be like his teacher. **Luke 6:40**

Tim wanted to look more and more like Jesus. We all are disciples of someone. Whose are you?

Like many of us, Tim just needed someone to believe in him. He needed someone to encourage him to step up and make a difference, to cheer him along. In time Tim would receive the highest praise any man received from Paul. Like a proud father Paul declared,

I have no one else like him. **Philippians 2:20**

This young disciple rose like a phoenix from the ashes of his difficult childhood to become faithful (1 Corinthians 4:17), genuine (Philippians 2:19, 20), proven (Philippians 2:22), a fellow worker (Romans 16:21) and a cherished "son" (1 Timothy 1:18).

Tim wasn't a super-spiritual giant we can't relate to. He was just a regular young guy. He was frequently ill (1 Timothy 5:23), may have been timid (2 Timothy 1:7), looked down on (1 Timothy 4:12) and fearful (1 Corinthians 16:10). On many occasions Paul had to fire him up and push him on (1 Timothy 4:12-16; 2 Timothy 1:6, 7). He struggled with weakness and temptation (2 Timothy 2:22). He struggled like all of us do. He had his bad days, his fears and his big, crazy, God-sized dreams. But he dedicated himself and rose to the challenge to take the gospel to his generation and to fellowship in the sufferings of Christ like a true disciple (Hebrews 13:23). He became the coauthor of six of Paul's epistles. At the end of Paul's life, when Paul was in prison, abandoned, cold, afraid and discouraged, he wanted only one person to come and comfort him . . . Timothy.

Only true disciples will have a pure passion to change history as Timothy did. So what does a disciple of Jesus look like?

Disciples Go the Way of the Cross

If any of you wants to be my follower, you must put aside your selfish ambition, shoulder your cross daily, and follow me. If you try to keep your life for yourself, you will lose it. But if you give up your life for me, you will find true life. . . . And you cannot be my disciple if you do not carry your own cross and follow me. Luke 9:23, 24; 14:27, NLT

What does the cross mean to us today? Is it a symbol of faith, a piece
of jewelry or a sign that all churches display, like McDonald's® golden
arches? When we hear the phrase *it's my cross to bear*, we often think of bear-
ing a burden, like a personal inconvenience, or some kind of suffering. But
what would the disciples have imagined when they heard these words for
the first time? In Jewish society, the punishment for a serious crime was for
the offender to be stoned. When the Greek Empire swept into Palestine,
they brought with them one of the most hideous forms of punishment
ever imagined—crucifixion. In fact, one of the most memorable events
involving crucifixion took place in Israel. A ruler named Alexander Janneus
captured 800 religious leaders and crucified them all at the same time, lin-
ing the main road entering Jerusalem with men on crosses. Anyone entering
Jerusalem would have walked a road that was lined on both sides—like a
street with telegraph poles—with 800 men nailed to 800 crosses, dying the
most agonizing death. It was a graphic, hideous image that surely would
have filled the disciples' minds as they heard Jesus' stark words.

Unlike the Greeks, the Roman Empire reserved crucifixion for the
worst criminals. It was the most cruel, horrible and humiliating death
imaginable. One thing was for sure: no one came down alive! So when Jesus
challenged the crowd to pick up their crosses, there was no confusion.
Suddenly the graphic images of the massacre at Jerusalem flooded their
minds. Just the thought was offensive. Did Jesus really mean that they were
to be rated with the worst of society? to humiliate their families and themselves and then slowly to die the most offensive and cruel death possible,
hanging naked as crowds poured out their scorn and made fun of them?
Were they really supposed to die like the worst criminals?

When Jesus asked the disciples to pick up their crosses, they did not
conjure up images of carrying a burden. When you picked up the cross, it
was a short walk . . . to your death. In our day and time Jesus might have
said, "If you are not willing to go to the electric chair . . . !" He said if you

are not willing to die, you are not worthy. So count the cost first—think about this before you do it. This is a serious commitment. You don't want to get into this, realize you underestimated the price, and look like a fool. He was so serious, he went on to give them two illustrations in Luke 14:28-33.

The first was of a man who told everyone he was going to build the world's tallest and biggest skyscraper but then ran out of money halfway through and ended up looking like a fool. The second story was of a man who went into battle against his enemy, only to find out his army was too small and he could not finish the job. Discipleship is a serious commitment; consider it carefully first. Jesus went on to say that if you lose your life, you will find it.

So what must we die to? We must die to our independent selves, to being in charge of our own lives, being our own masters. Jesus called for a total surrender of control to him. From now on, he must be the master and we the servants—it is all or nothing. The cross meant death to self. Jesus said that if we follow him, we must assume the role of a servant just as he did (Matthew 20:28). The concept of being a servant or slave is such a foundational part of his message that it is recorded in the Gospels on at least eighteen separate occasions. Let me give some perspective to that. Heaven is a foundational image in Christianity. We hear sermons on it, read books and buy tapes concerning it; you may even have a picture of someone's rendition of it on your living room wall. Yet there are only three or four occasions when Jesus mentioned our being in Heaven with him. This is in pretty stark contrast to the eighteen times he commands us to be servants. The first step in discipleship is your death to self. Here are a few areas in Timothy's life that underwent death to self.

1. Freedom

Could you imagine how nervous and scared Tim felt the first time he and Paul were arrested? the swirl of fear that went coursing through his body as the authorities pushed and shouted at them and threw them into a dark, smelly, rat-infested jail cell? Would they ever see the light of freedom again? What on earth would his mom think if she knew about this? He hated to think how she would respond. Perhaps it would be better if she didn't know. How long that first night must have seemed as Tim huddled in a corner and listened to the rats scrape and hunt down the cockroaches in the darkness. He could feel disease and discomfort wrap their cold, clammy fingers around him, and he shivered. Did his time in jail last for days, weeks or months? One thing was for sure when he finally stepped out again into the warm sunshine beyond his cell—he knew he would be back. With Paul, Tim was no stranger to jail sentences. He too knew what it was like to be beaten and to sleep outside in the cold rain or sweltering heat. Timothy had to give up the basic right to do what he wanted when he wanted. Perhaps it was college, a career, a girlfriend or simply the ability to walk as a free man.

Wait a minute. That was just for people in Timothy's day, right? Today we live in a free world. It's one of our basic rights, isn't it? Many have given their lives fighting and struggling for the freedom we enjoy today. While our freedom is a gift to be cherished, it is also a gift we must be willing to give back to God. We need to hold it with an open hand, not a clenched first. It doesn't mean God necessarily wants to take our rights away; it's about our heart attitude. We need an attitude that says, "Lord, you are more important to me than this."

The fear of giving up our freedoms can often keep us from obeying God's will. Could dislike of the food in a certain country keep you from following God there? What if they don't eat hamburgers in that country? What if there is not a bed—could you sleep on the floor? Would you give up your desire for a good night's sleep, warmth, air conditioning or TV?

When Tim laid down his right to his freedom, the jail became a mission field and he had a captive audience! They were not really prisoners; they were right where God wanted them to be. A missionary named Jim Elliot once said, "He is no fool who gives what he cannot keep to gain what he cannot lose." You can trust Jesus. As Timothy laid down his life, he found out what it meant to really live.

> ### *Any of you who does not give up everything he has cannot be my disciple.*
> **Luke 14:33**

You can't just follow Jesus when it is socially acceptable or when you're hungry for a free lunch. Someone once said Jesus is either Lord of all or not at all. You have to count the cost and lay everything on the altar. This is why Jesus said to think about it, to make sure you are ready. Is there anything you are still holding onto—anything you are not willing to give up? Are you willing to hold all your freedoms with an open hand and allow God to take them back if he wants to? What about your freedom to have a boyfriend or girlfriend, or your freedom to choose your own college or career path? Timothy wanted God more than anything else. He gave up his rights to all these things, holding them in an open palm. I don't think he had any regrets. Until you have died to everything, you are not free to do anything.

2. Family

Tim's mind often drifted back home, especially during difficult times when he and Paul had no money, nothing to eat or nowhere to sleep. He would wonder what his friends were doing. They probably had normal lives. They could hang out on Friday evenings and go to a ball game on the weekends. He missed his granny and, of course, he missed his mom. How many nights did he go to sleep hungry and dream of mom's cooking? It was always hardest during the holidays. He knew all his uncles, aunts and cousins would soon arrive at home, and oh man, the food . . . !

If anyone comes to me and does not hate his father and mother, his wife and children, his brothers and sisters—yes, even his own life—he cannot be my disciple. And anyone who does not carry his cross and follow me cannot be my disciple. . . . In the same way, any of you who does not give up everything he has cannot be my disciple. **Luke 14:26, 27, 33**

Does Jesus literally mean we should hate our moms and dads? I don't think so, although you may have a brother or sister you would like to use this Scripture on right now! Jesus was calling his disciples to love and be committed to him above anything else, even family and friends. Are you willing to hold your family and friends with an open hand? Are you willing to give up having a boyfriend or girlfriend? If you are single, are you willing to give up your right to be married? If you are married, are you willing to give up your right to have a family? Are you willing to give up your right to be close to family and friends, even during the holidays?

That's radical and it's tough. There will be times when your family and friends don't understand. There will be times when they think you have abandoned them, that you care more about total strangers than them, that you hate them. Sometimes people just don't understand, but Jesus calls us to radical obedience.

3. Comfort

But you, Timothy, belong to God; so run from all these evil things, and follow what is right and good. Pursue a godly life, along with faith, love,

perseverance, and gentleness. Fight the good fight for what we believe.
Hold tightly to the eternal life that God has given you.

1 Timothy 6:11, 12, NLT

....

In these verses Paul used four words to describe the life of a disciple: *run, pursue, fight* and *hold*. It sounds like one of those epic battles where the hero struggles on to victory against all odds. He is outsized, outmuscled and out-armed, but after being beaten to within an inch of his life, he somehow focuses all his energy and strength to mount the comeback of the century. But wait a minute—that's not usually the picture of Christianity that's communicated to us by those shiny preachers on TV. The life of a disciple is a life of discipline and diligence. Paul called Tim to

....

Join with me in suffering for the gospel. **2 Timothy 1:8**

....

You don't often hear that line at youth gatherings these days. It's at times when we must run from temptation, when we feel an overwhelming desire to give in, that we must fight and hold tightly—even though we feel like giving in and giving up. It's when Christianity doesn't seem to make any sense or any difference that we grow spiritually.

The first thing we need is a strong foundation of obedience.

....

Therefore everyone who hears these words of mine and puts them into
practice is like a wise man who built his house on the rock.

Matthew 7:24

....

That foundation has to be the Word of God in our lives. Jesus did not say that *hearing* the word would lay a foundation in our lives. We must put

it into practice. This is one of the key differences between disciples and followers. Obedience is the foundation stone. We are building on the rock only if we are walking in obedience to God's commands. You may know God's Word, but if you are not obediently doing it, you are building on sand. When the storms of life blow, you're going down.

Secondly, as we move in obedience, we must keep our eyes fixed on Jesus.

Let us strip off every weight that slows us down, especially the sin that so easily hinders our progress. And let us run with endurance the race that God has set before us. We do this by keeping our eyes on Jesus, on whom our faith depends from start to finish. **Hebrews 12:1, 2, NLT**

You've all been to the stadium and seen the athletes race. Everyone runs; one wins. Run to win. All good athletes train hard. They do it for a gold medal that tarnishes and fades. You're after one that's gold eternally.
1 Corinthians 9:24, 25, THE MESSAGE

The life of a disciple is a race, but it's a marathon and not a sprint. A marathon is as much a test of mental fitness as of physical fitness. In a marathon, around mile 16 your body and mind hit a stage called the wall. You just want to stop and give up. Unless you can push through, you will not finish the race. The Christian life is like this. As we run we will hit walls that will drain us of our passion and energy. We will feel like giving up unless we cast off anything that is weighing us down. This takes a commitment to fix our eyes on the finish line and run to win. If you are going to bother getting all sweaty, why not run to win the prize?

Thirdly, realize that these challenges purify us and cause us to grow.

Dear brothers and sisters, whenever trouble comes your way, let it be an opportunity for joy. For when your faith is tested, your endurance has a chance to grow. So let it grow, for when your endurance is fully developed, you will be strong in character and ready for anything.

James 1:2-4, NLT

Trials are hard, but they are not pointless. God is concerned for our best. He is so committed to our best, he is willing to walk through the hardships with us. It is the confirmation of God's working in our lives (Hebrews 12:7-11) to produce growth and maturity. We all want to have mountaintop experiences, right? Have you ever been on a mountaintop? What was up there? I have never seen crops growing on a mountaintop. I have never found a grove of fruit trees or a vineyard. Fruit is grown in the valleys below. We think of the valley experiences as the difficult times of life. But it's where the fruit is produced.

Timothy had to follow Jesus, which meant dying to himself. There were times when he had to leave Paul or spend many lonely nights on the road or in strange cities. He had to learn to eat different foods. He missed his friends. There were times when he had to stand up against older people, times when he had to get away for fear that he might look back and get off track. There were times when he felt afraid and unsure, times when he almost gave up. But Timothy counted the cost and loved Jesus more than freedom, family, comfort, earthly desires and even self. He made the sacrifice because he wanted the destiny God had for him—to be part of what God was doing—more than anything else. What about you?

Making Waves

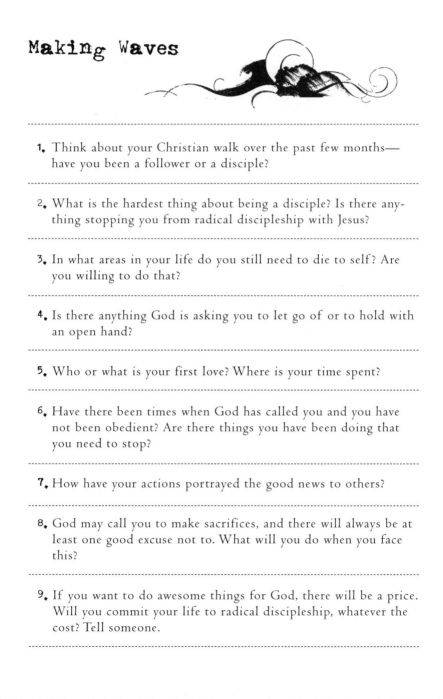

1. Think about your Christian walk over the past few months—have you been a follower or a disciple?

2. What is the hardest thing about being a disciple? Is there anything stopping you from radical discipleship with Jesus?

3. In what areas in your life do you still need to die to self? Are you willing to do that?

4. Is there anything God is asking you to let go of or to hold with an open hand?

5. Who or what is your first love? Where is your time spent?

6. Have there been times when God has called you and you have not been obedient? Are there things you have been doing that you need to stop?

7. How have your actions portrayed the good news to others?

8. God may call you to make sacrifices, and there will always be at least one good excuse not to. What will you do when you face this?

9. If you want to do awesome things for God, there will be a price. Will you commit your life to radical discipleship, whatever the cost? Tell someone.

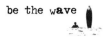
List three things God has shown you in this chapter that you don't want to forget.

1.

2.

3.

Be the Wave

Lord, from this moment on I commit to . . .

Spend a few minutes talking to God about how you feel. List some specific prayer points that will help you live out the truths in this chapter.

what now?

It wasn't that long ago that I was planted facedown in the hole with Gideon. I lacked courage, conviction or calling. Until, that is, God showed up and challenged me to dare to believe his furious love and crazy destiny for me. If God is challenging you to dial down the static of the world that buzzes in your thoughts telling you you'll never amount to anything, I encourage you to dare to believe and chase after the amazing plans he has for you. You have a destiny that is unlike anything the world has ever seen, heard of or imagined before (1 Corinthians 2:9).

One way to begin that journey is to consider dedicating six months to God at Youth with a Mission on a Discipleship Training School (DTS). A DTS is a life-changing experience to help you "know God and to make him known." It is a time for you to seek God's face, hear his voice and discover your destiny! Putting aside all the distractions of life, you can focus on Jesus and hear his heartbeat for the nations. It's a time to step out of your comfort zone and give God your whole heart—your whole life! It's time to know God's heart for a hurting world and see him use *you* to reach those who are bruised and dying. I guarantee that after the experience, you will be spoiled for the ordinary.

If you would like more information about a DTS or about joining us for a short-term missions outreach, you can contact us through our Web site: www.ywamwaves.com or write to me personally at: hensser@hotmail.com.

Dream.

Draw.

reflect.

sanctuary
a journal to download my ideas,
remember experiences,
draw and dream . . .

02957

canvas
a journal to download my ideas,
remember experiences,
draw and dream . . .

02956

sacrifice
a journal to download my ideas,
remember experiences,
draw and dream . . .

02958

BEYOND

a journal

COMPILED BY LYNN LUSBY PRATT
AUTHOR OF DEVOTIONS BY DEAD PEOPLE

02900

spiral-bound
art journals
for you to
take reflective
refuge from
the world and
express what
God is doing in
your life.

also from standard publishing . . .

Appointments with God series

Each of these two books includes 150 daily encounters with God. Meet with God each day and discover his incredible promises, his character and his love for you.

- Getting to Know God
- Getting to Know Jesus
- Getting to Know His Word

Order # 23327

- Getting to Know Myself
- Getting to Know My Friends
- Getting to Know Others

Order # 23328

Available at your local Christian bookstore or from Standard Publishing at 1.800.543.1353.
www.standardpub.com

refuge™

ref·uge \'re-fyüj
shelter or protection from danger or distress

*"My salvation and my honor come from God alone.
He is my refuge, a rock where no enemy can reach me.
O my people, trust in him at all times.
Pour out your heart to him,
for God is our refuge."*
—*Psalm 62: 7, 8, NLT*

In the Old Testament God provided six "cities of refuge" where a person could seek safe haven from vengeance. These cities were places of protection. Today refuge™ will provide you the safe haven you need to grow in your relationship with God.

rfg   www.rfgbooks.com